P9-BIN-032

WOMAN ABUSE
Sociological Perspectives

WOMAN ABUSE

Sociological Perspectives

Walter S. DeKeseredy
Carleton University

Ronald Hinch
University of Guelph

Thompson Educational Publishing, Inc.
Toronto, Ontario / Lewiston, New York

Copyright © 1991 Walter S. DeKeseredy and Ronald Hinch

All rights reserved. No part of this publication may be reproduced or transmitted in any form or by any means, electronic or mechanical, including photocopy, recording, or any information storage and retrieval system, without permission in writing from the publisher.

Requests for permission to make copies of any part of this work should be sent to the publisher.

Canadian Cataloguing in Publication Data
DeKeseredy, Walter S., 1959–
 Woman abuse

Includes bibliographical references and index.
ISBN 1–55077–032–2

1. Women – Canada – Crimes against. 2. Wife abuse – Canada.   I. Hinch, Ronald Owen.
II. Title.

HV6250.4W65D4   1991   364.1'53'0971   C91–094422–9

ISBN 1–55077–032–2 Paper

Printed in Canada.
 2 3 4 5   94 93 92

TABLE OF CONTENTS

AUGUSTANA UNIVERSITY COLLEGE
LIBRARY

For Patricia DeKeseredy and Peggy-Ann Hinch

ACKNOWLEDGEMENTS

Many friends and colleagues helped us write this book. We are especially indebted to the following people who took time away from their busy schedules to read and critique portions of the manuscript: Gregg Barak, Jacquelyn Campbell, Tullio Caputo, Dawn Currie, Jurgen Dankwort, Colin Goff, Katharine Kelly, Martin Schwartz, Michael D. Smith, and the three anonymous reviewers of Chapters 4 and 5. Their comments made this book better than it otherwise would have been. We are also grateful to Desmond Ellis, Alan Hunt, Holly Johnson, Brian MacLean, Fernando Mata, and John Myles for providing additional help with various issues addressed in this manuscript. Of course, we assume full responsibility for any errors which appear here.

Special thanks go to Ann Carroll, Nazira Conroy, Lynn Gunn, Eva Hegmann, Kim Mitchell, and Jennifer Quaile. Their contributions to the completion of this project are too numerous to mention.

The support of Carleton University is also greatly appreciated. Financial assistance provided by the Faculty of Graduate Studies and Research, and by the office of the Dean of Social Sciences helped us collect information on various topics included in *Woman Abuse: Sociological Perspectives*.

Finally, we want to thank Keith Thompson for his patience, cooperation, and editorial assistance.

1

INTRODUCTION

Since the early 1970s, thanks to the feminist movement, there has been an enormous growth in the amount of public and professional attention given to wife-beating in Western capitalist societies. Prior to this time, many women "suffered in silence" (Pizzey, 1974). Despite a higher level of awareness, many people are still uninformed about the types and amount of abuse that women experience in marital relationships. On the other hand, many recognize that wife assault is endemic to many families, but they choose to ignore it for a variety of reasons.[1]

Nevertheless, "atrocity tales" (Goffman, 1961) about both the psychological and physical pain that husbands inflict on their spouses are now commonplace in television shows, newspaper reports, and feature films (Messerschmidt, 1986).[2] In addition, thousands of academic journal articles and hundreds of scholarly books on husband-to-wife violence are published every year. In fact, advances in the social scientific study of this problem have been faster paced than some of the major developments in the physical sciences (Schwartz and DeKeseredy, 1988).

Given this rapid increase in attention, many people believe that violence against wives is a relatively new social problem. Linked to this perception is the dominant belief among the North American public, media personnel, and social commentators that we are presently experiencing an "epidemic" of wife assault (Gelles and Straus, 1988). Both of these contentions are incorrect because violence against wives has existed for centuries (Dobash and Dobash, 1979; Okun, 1986). Although

---

[1] Two of the most common explanations for this "selective inattention" (Dexter, 1958) are because: (1) family issues are often perceived as private rather than public matters (Pahl, 1985) and (2) many people blame victims for their mistreatment (Okun, 1986).

[2] A salient example of the large amount of media attention given to woman-battering in recent years is the Lisa Steinberg murder case. For more information on this tragic story, see Ehrlich (1989).

TABLE 1-1: Woman Abuse: A Typology

Victim	Nature of Offence
Wife	Physical and sexual assault; psychological abuse; economic cruelty.
Dating partner	Physical and sexual assault; psychological abuse.
Cohabitor	Physical and sexual assault; psychological abuse; economic cruelty.
Separated and divorced women	Physical and sexual assault; psychological abuse; economic cruelty.
Consumer	Injuries and deaths resulting from unsafe products (e.g., Dalkon Shield, tampons, DES).
Employee	Deaths and injuries in the workplace (e.g., exposure to hazardous wastes and electromagnetic radiation); sexual harassment.

researchers cannot conclusively state that wife abuse is not on the rise, historical data suggest that today's husbands are no more violent, and possibly slightly less violent, than their ancestors (Straus et al., 1981).

Social scientists now have a substantial body of knowledge on the sources and consequences of many forms of wife-beating. They have also demystified some popular myths and stereotypes about this problem. However, they have very little knowledge on marital rape. Furthermore, compared to what they know about nonsexual abuse among married women, they know relatively little about male violence toward women in other marital status categories; especially separated and divorced women (Ellis and DeKeseredy, 1989).

Researchers know even less about violent "crimes of capital" committed against females in the workplace and in other contexts. These offenses are, according to Michalowski (1985: 314), " ... socially injurious acts that arise from the ownership or management of capital or from occupancy of positions of trust in institutions designed to facilitate the accumulation of capital." Research shows that dangerous health products such as the Dalkon Shield and various pharmaceuticals have hurt a substantial number of people (Cullen et al., 1987; McDonnell, 1986). Many women also face major health hazards in jobs often referred to as "female ghettos" (CACSW, 1976; Reasons et al., 1981). In addition, a large number of females experience secondary victimization at the hands of a male-dominated state[3] which often fails to provide them with adequate social support and protection (DeKeseredy, 1988a). A modified version of Goff and Reason's (1986) typology of organizational crimes presents some of the most salient types of offenses and victim groups (see Table 1-1).

Table 1-1 shows that women are victims of a wide range of offenses in a variety of social contexts. Thus, a research agenda that limits its focus to physical assaults in the marital home offers an inadequate understanding of the pain and suffering women endure in Western countries such as Canada, Britain and the U.S.

In summary, although researchers have contributed significantly to an understanding of wife abuse, they have excluded a wide range of crimes that are equally, if not more, harmful to women. Thus, there is clearly an urgent need for a broader research agenda that examines the multidimensional nature of woman abuse.

Consistent with previous attempts to expand the boundaries of both victimology and criminology (Schwendinger and Schwendinger, 1970; Michalowski, 1985; Elias, 1986; Young and Reasons, 1989; Young, 1988), the principal objective of this book is to provide a broad-based, analysis of woman abuse in Canada. We examine not only the problem of wife-beating, but many other forms of female victimization. A comprehensive, critical overview of theoretical and empirical literature on the following issues is provided: wife abuse, premarital woman abuse, rape and sexual assault, and corporate crimes of violence. The strengths and weakness of various policies aimed at curbing each of these problems are also discussed. Similar to one of the major goals of the "new victimology," we hope that our approach will " ... raise victim consciousness and pursue new, social justice concerns" (Elias, 1986: 25).

The secondary purpose of this book is to instill a sociological understanding of female victimization. A sociological perspective " ... focuses on the way in which individual behaviour is influenced, conditioned, shaped, constrained, or determined by their social relationships to other human beings and to a variety of social institutions" (Eitzen and Timmer, 1985: 6). Since woman abuse is endemic to Western, post-industrial societies (Dobash and Dobash, 1979), and occurs in all major social and

---

[3] For the purpose of this book, Miliband's (1969: 50) definition of the state is employed. The state consists of the following components: the government, the bureaucracy, the military, the judiciary, the subcentral government, and parliamentary assemblies.

demographic groups (Smith, 1990), it cannot be explained adequately by biological or psychological perspectives (Pagelow, 1981). In fact, it is estimated that only 10 percent of all wife and abuse cases are caused by mental disorders (Gelles and Straus, 1988). Thus, woman abuse is a "public issue" rather than a "personal trouble" (Mills, 1959; DeKeseredy, 1988a).

Like some feminists (e.g., Bograd, 1988), we recognize that a small number of abusive men are psychopathological. However, given the high incidence and prevalence rates reported in Canada and other countries[4], we reject nonsociological perspectives because they:

> ... ignore the question of power. They cannot answer the question of why allegedly mentally ill men beat their wives and not their bosses, nor why impulse ridden, out of control husbands contain their rage until they are in the privacy of their homes, at which time they bruise their wives but less frequently kill them (Bograd, 1988: 17).

Linked to these problems is the fact that policies derived from nonsociological theories are fraught with limitations. For example, because psychological and biological theorists view violent crime as a property of the individual, they have supported conservatives' repressive attempts to adjust offenders to the dominant social order through strategies such as punishment, medical and psychiatric treatment, counseling or other individualistic control methods (Timmer and Eitzen, 1989).[5] Since woman abuse, however, is a specific result of capitalist economic conditions interacting with patriarchal social relations (Messerschmidt, 1986; Schwartz and DeKeseredy, 1988), these initiatives have failed (and will continue to fail) to stop woman abuse (Pence and Shepard, 1988; Eitzen and Timmer, 1985; Currie, 1985).

Capitalism refers to a political economic system that is based on the exploitation of the working class by the capitalist class which owns and controls the means of production (e.g., factories, companies, financial corporations, etc.).[6] There is no precise definition of patriarchy. In fact, defining this concept has caused a major debate in the feminist literature (Messerschmidt, 1986). Following Eisenstein (1980: 16), patriarchy is re-

---

[4] See Pahl (1985), Campbell (1985), and Levinson (1989) for summaries of cross-cultural studies.

[5] For a more detailed discussion on conservative crime control strategies and their limitations, see Currie (1985), Messerschmidt (1986), and Eitzen and Timmer (1985).

[6] This is a modified version of Quinney's (1977) definition of capitalism.

ferred to here as " ... a sexual system of power in which the male possesses superior power and economic privilege." Some researchers assert that there are two types of patriarchy: "social" and "familial" (Smith, in press). The former refers to male domination at the societal level and the latter refers to male control in the home (Barrett, 1980; Eisenstein, 1980; Ursel, 1984, 1986; Smith, in press).

In sharp contrast to psychologists and biologists, sociologists propose policies that address the social sources of woman abuse and other types of violent crime. Nevertheless, as will be demonstrated in subsequent chapters, the sociological perspective is not a unified enterprise. A variety of policies derived from different sociological explanations (e.g., subcultural, social support, and resource theories) have been proposed to deal with the substantive problems examined throughout this book. Although we attempt to give each orientation equal attention and a fair assessment, we personally adhere to a progressive or radical sociological school of thought.

Progressives call for strategies that target the wider political and economic forces that influence men to harm women in a variety of social contexts. Some radicals may be referred to as "idealists" since they contend that only a transformation to a socialist feminist, anti-racist society will end woman abuse (Schwartz and DeKeseredy, 1991). Short-term initiatives are repudiated by left idealists because they believe that social and criminal justice reforms: (1) lend support to repressive state practices; (2) destroy informal systems of social control (Young, 1986); (3) do not eliminate the inequalities of capitalism and patriarchy which are major sources of female victimization (Schwartz and DeKeseredy, 1991; Lynch and Groves, 1989); and (4) delay the revolution (Collins, 1984).[7]

The notion that woman abuse and other types of predatory street crime will not be eliminated until there is a fundamental change in the structure of society is common to another strand of progressive sociological thought—left realism. Unlike left idealists, however, left realists (e.g., Lea and Young, 1984; Matthews and Young, 1986; Kinsey et al., 1986; Currie, 1985) assert that various reforms are required prior to the revolution because it is unlikely to occur in the near future (Messerschmidt, 1986).

According to left realists, the idealist "abstentionist position" on short-term initiatives (Boehringer et al., 1983) is " ... too visionary or utopian" (Eitzen and Timmer, 1985: 575). Moreover, they argue that left-wing

---

[7] For a more detailed discussion on the principles and limitations of left idealism, see Young (1979, 1986) and Schwartz and DeKeseredy (1991).

selective inattention allows right-wing politicians to use the "law and order" issue to manufacture ideological support for a social order detrimental to the powerless and the construction of a socialist feminist society (Taylor, 1982; Schwartz and DeKeseredy, 1991; MacLean and DeKeseredy, 1990).

Left realists propose strategies that "chip away" (Messerschmidt, 1986) at patriarchal capitalism. Examples of these "middle range policy initiatives which do not compromise any overall design for fundamental social change ... " (Cohen, 1979: 49) are: (1) demarginalization; (2) preemptive deterrence; democratic control of the police; (3) community participation in crime prevention and policy development; (4) employment programs; and (5) social services (Lea and Young, 1984; Currie, 1989). More detailed discussions on the effectiveness of some of these (and other) policy proposals are found throughout this book.

Like other perspectives, left realism has shortcomings[8]. Nevertheless, since it attempts to immediately challenge the major sources of woman abuse, patriarchy and capitalism, it is an important alternative to both left idealist abstentionism and the ineffective, repressive crime control polices inherent to individualistic, predispositional theories.

Since most of the sociological studies on woman abuse and its control have been conducted in the U.S. and the U.K., this book has a decidedly Canadian focus. There is a great shortage of theoretical and empirical research on female victimization in Canada. Thus, we hope that this book will help fill a vacuum in the Canadian victimological literature.

Outline

Each substantive topic discussed in this book has a chapter to itself. Chapter 2 covers wife abuse; Chapter 3 addresses premarital woman abuse; Chapter 4 deals with rape and sexual assault; and Chapter 5 with corporate violence. Each chapter begins with a definition of the substantive topic being examined. Following this discussion is a description of the incidence and distribution of the subject. Then relevant theories and policies are discussed. All of these chapters conclude with a summary. The last chapter, Chapter 6, is devoted to conclusions.

---

[8] See Scraton (1987), Schwartz and DeKeseredy (1991); and DeKeseredy and Schwartz (in press-a, in press-b) for comprehensive critiques of left realism.

2

WIFE ABUSE

What is wife abuse? What is its extent and distribution? What causes men to beat their wives? What can we do to stop men assaulting women in conjugal relationships? There are no widely accepted answers to these questions and perhaps a consensus can never be reached among the Canadian public, agents of social control, and sociologists. The primary purpose of this chapter is to critically review major sociological responses to the above four questions. Before we focus on these issues, however, it is necessary to answer another important question, "who is a wife?"

Who Is a Wife?

For the purpose of this book, a wife is any woman who is legally married or is sexually and emotionally linked to a male cohabiter.[1] This definition is offered for four reasons. One, it is similar to others employed in previous Canadian woman abuse research (Smith, 1990). Second, there are few differences between cohabiting and married women (Yllo and Straus, 1981). For example, like married women, cohabiters are less likely than their partners to initiate sexual activity, rarely make spending decisions, and do much more housework than their mates, even if both of them have jobs (Blumestein and Schwartz, 1983). Thus, common-law partners are similar to women legally designated as wives because they tend not to violate patriarchal gender norms (Blumestein and Schwartz, 1983; Lewin, 1982).[2]

---

[1] This is a revised version of Ellis' (1989) definition of cohabitation.

[2] Cohabiting women, however, tend to be younger than married females, and are less likely to have children (Turcotte, 1990).

A third reason for grouping cohabiters together with married women is that under certain conditions, such as in lengthy relationships and having children, cohabiters are subject to the same laws as married women (Mandell, 1987; Teevan, 1987). Hence, legal factors make many cohabiting relationships similar to marriage rather than extensions of the dating process.[3]

Finally, married and unmarried women report comparable levels of marital satisfaction and emotional closeness. They also experience similar conflicts and problems (Mandell, 1987).

Despite the strong rationale for our definition, some sociologists contend that it is problematic for the following reasons. First, Eshleman (1978) and Fels (1981), assert that many couples view cohabitation simply as an extension of the dating process. For these people, the major difference between "serious" premarital relationships and cohabiting is that cohabiters live under the same roof. Unmarried cohabitation is seen as offering more privacy than an undergraduate dormitory or parents' homes, and easier access to a sexual partner.

Second, many dating partners live with each other because of financial considerations rather than a desire to participate in "trial marriages." For example, many men prefer physical separation from their partners; however, the high cost of living in large, metropolitan areas (e.g., Toronto, Montreal, and Vancouver) encouraged them to enter cohabiting relationships (Stein, 1983).

Third, Rosenblatt and Budd (1975) found that cohabiters and married couples differ significantly in their perceptions of territoriality and privacy. Cohabiters were more likely to challenge marriage norms that oppose physical separateness and that promote togetherness. In addition, cohabiters, unlike married persons, tend to maintain other residences as well as have places within the cohabiting home for privacy. Based on these findings, Rosenblatt and Budd argue that cohabitation is not similar to marriage and is an advanced type of courtship.

Fourth, unlike married women, many cohabiters do not want a formal legal arrangement (Eshleman, 1978). Instead, they look for a permanent, nonbinding union that allows them the freedom to leave their partners without legal responsibility.

To sum up, there is a great amount of disagreement over who is and who is not a wife. Our view, however, is that is difficult to differentiate

---

[3]   In Canada, limited legal rights were given to female cohabiters to protect them from exploitive relationships and to lower social assistance costs. The provinces are responsible for governing cohabitation (Mandell, 1987).

between cohabiters and legally married women. Thus, our definition includes both groups.

What Is Wife Abuse?

According to Ellis (1987a), debates surrounding this question focus mainly on three issues that incorporate both political and technical concerns. These are: (1) the breadth of definitions (broad versus narrow), (2) objectivity versus subjectivity and (3) terminology (gender-neutral versus gender-specific terms).

The Breadth of Definitions

There is considerable disagreement about what harmful acts should be included in a definitions of wife abuse. Most Canadian researchers (e.g., Brinkerhoff and Lupri, 1988; Dutton, 1988; Kennedy and Dutton, 1989; Smith, 1985, 1986, 1987, 1989a, 1990, in press) restrict their focus to physical violence. Gelles and Cornell (1985: 23) contend that definitions which are confined to physical behaviours are necessary because "...lumping all forms of malevolence and harm-doing together may muddy the water so much that it might be impossible to determine what causes abuse."

By only focusing on physical assaults, researchers apparently assume that these acts are worse than psychological abuse (Breines and Gordon, 1983; DeKeseredy and MacLean, 1991). Many women strongly disagree with this position. For example, U.S. researcher Lenore Walker (1979) reports that most of her female subjects described incidents of psychological humiliation and verbal harassment as their worst abusive experiences, regardless of whether they had been physically attacked. Based on these findings and other studies (e.g., Denzin, 1984; MacLeod, 1987), some Canadian researchers provide definitions which emphasize both violent and psychologically abusive behaviours (Lupri and Price, 1990).

Since many Canadian women who are beaten are also economically and sexually victimized by their partners, MacLeod (1987) and Stark-Adamec and Adamec (1982) contend that all of the above definitions are too limited. They clearly recognize the multidimensional nature of wife abuse. Many violent episodes are often preceded by psychological assaults or "economic violence," such as withholding money for groceries (MacLeod, 1987). Moreover, many women are both verbally abused and beaten before they are raped (Browne, 1987). In fact, according to Frieze (1983: 552), " ... marital rape is typically associated with battering and may be one of the most serious forms of battering."[4] Sexual abuse is addressed in Chapter 4 and thus it will not be discussed further here. However, the economic abuse of wives is not given much attention in this book mainly because of the limited amount of Canadian research on this problem. Most of the information on "economic brutality" is anecdotal (e.g., MacLeod, 1987). Hopefully, researchers will attempt to gather more accurate data because acts of economic cruelty have major implications for the health and welfare of women and their children.

The pain and suffering caused by one common form of economic wife abuse, withholding money, is described by one of MacLeod's respondents (1987: 17):

> I used to think that his total control over the money was just a quirk, wasn't worth worrying about. After all, I was at home with the kids all day and I usually had $2 or $3 that he'd leave me. I didn't really need any more. Then one day he went away on a business trip for a week. He bought us some groceries before he went and left me with $10 for the whole week, to feed me and three kids, saying with a smirk that I'd better make it last, because it's all I would get. Well, we ran out of food after three days and we nearly starved trying to feed me and three kids on $10 for four days. But the worst was that my middle boy got hit in the mouth with a stick and should have gotten stitches, but I didn't even have the bus fare to take him to the hospital and I was scared of what my husband would do if I asked a neighbour for money.

Objective Versus Subjective Definitions

Ellis (1987a) contends that most sociologists define woman abuse objectively. For example, even if an abusive husband is not officially or publicly designated as a wife-beater, he is usually defined as one by researchers. Subjective definitions of crime and deviance, such as the following, are generally repudiated by sociological students of woman abuse:

> ... deviance is not a quality of the act the person commits, but rather a consequence of the application by others of rules and sanctions to an "offender." The deviant is one to whom that label has successfully

---

[4] Browne (1987) states that researchers incorrectly separate "sexual" from "physical abuse."

been applied; deviant behaviour is behaviour that people so label (Becker, 1987: 10).

According to this assertion, men who secretly beat their partners are not really woman abusers because they have not been publicly identified.

The rejection of the societal reaction definition is based on political considerations.[5] According to Ellis (1987a: 160):

> Thus, to call a man who assaults his wife a wife abuser is to show greater support for women and greater opposition to violence against women than would be the case if one were to limit this term (wife abuser) only to wife assaulters who have been publicly identified as wife abusers.

Terminology[6]

Most abuse among North American couples involves men beating, raping or psychologically mistreating (or a combination of all three)[7] their partners (Okun, 1986). Of course some women physically assault men; however, female violence, even with the intent to injure, is used primarily in self-defence (Berk et al., 1983; Browne, 1987; Dobash and Dobash, 1988; Makepeace, 1986; Saunders, 1986, 1988, 1989). Furthermore, many women who initiate attacks hit first because of a "well-founded fear" (Hamner and Saunders, 1984) of being beaten or raped by their partners (Saunders, 1989). Both physical and sexual attacks are often preceded by name-calling and other types of psychological abuse (Browne, 1987). These early warning signs prompt many women to hit first in order to deter their partners from hitting them (Saunders, 1989). Thus, most assaults initiated by women may actually be acts of self-defence (DeKescredy, in press).

A few scholars question the validity of these findings. They assert that marital and cohabiting violence is a "two way street" and that many men experience "husband abuse" (McNeely and Robinson-Simpson, 1987; Steinmetz, 1977–78; Straus, 1989; Stets and Straus, 1990). Therefore, they define abuse in gender-neutral terms (Breines and Gordon, 1983). Definitions such as "marital violence," "spousal violence," "domestic vio-

---

5 Even eminent symbolic interactionist Edwin Schur provides an objective definition of woman abuse in his subjectively oriented book entitled *Labelling Women Deviant* (1984: 157).

6 For a comprehensive discussion on the politics of terminology, see Walker (1990).

7 For example, Russell (1975: 82–83) describes an incident in which a man spent an entire day insulting his partner. Following this abuse, he beat and sodomized her.

lence," and "spouse abuse" are often used by scholars who provide an inaccurate, "mutual combat" (Berk et al., 1983), image of violence in intimate relationships. They are also used by many U.S. researchers; especially those affiliated with the University of New Hampshire's Family Violence Research Program (e.g., Finkelhor et al., 1988; Gelles, 1979; Straus et al., 1981; Straus, 1989). In Canada, some sociologists use one or more of the above definitions (Chan, 1978; Chimbos, 1978; Fleming, 1975; Prus, 1978; Brinkerhoff and Lupri, 1988).

Terms such as marital violence have many limitations. First, they are ideological constructs which conceal the fact that women are more frequently and seriously abused by men (Box, 1983; Small, 1981; Walker, 1990). Second, gender-neutral phrases do not address who initiates the violence, variance in physical strength and fighting competence between men and women, the extent of willingness to use this strength and whether violence is in self-defence (Freedman, 1985).

Third, gender-neutral definitions have major implications for the treatment of female victims. If state officials believe that women are just as violent as men, they may not provide battered women with adequate social support. For example, Steinmetz's (1977–78) incorrect assertion that husband beating is as prevalent as wife beating was used by Chicago state officials to block funding for a shelter for abused women and their children (Pleck et al., 1977–78). Like battered women in Chicago, Canadian women could suffer from state indifference caused indirectly by gender-neutral definitions (DeKeseredy, 1988a).

Most Canadian sociologists recognize the pitfalls of definitions that portray male-female relationships as mutually violent. These researchers also argue that women are the main victims of assault in domestic relationships. Thus, they use the following terms: wife-battering (Burris and Jaffe, 1984; MacLeod, 1980), wife assault (Small, 1981; Freedman, 1985; Kennedy and Dutton, 1989; Scott, 1990), wife abuse (Ellis, 1987a, Jaffe et al., 1986; Ursel and Farough, 1986; Ursel, 1990; Johnson, 1990; Smith, 1990), wife beating (MacLeod, 1987; Smith, in press), woman abuse (Smith, 1985, 1986, 1987, 1989a, 1989b; DeKeseredy and MacLean, 1991; Ellis and DeKeseredy, 1989) and wife battery (Currie, 1990; Currie and MacLean, in press).

In sum, the sociology of wife abuse is characterized by a wide range of definitions. We provide one that is broad in scope, objective, and clearly identifies women as the principal victims of abuse in conjugal contexts. Throughout this chapter, wife abuse refers to any intentional physical or psychological assault on a woman by a husband or a male cohabiter. The term physical assault covers a wide range of violent behaviours, from pushing and shoving to murder (Gelles and Straus, 1988). A psychological assault is any act:

> ... intended to cause psychological pain to another person, or a communication perceived as having that intent. The communicative act may be active or passive, and verbal or non-verbal. Examples include name calling or nasty remarks (active, verbal), slamming a door or smashing something (active, non-verbal), and stony silence or sulking (passive, non-verbal) (Straus et al., 1989).

Conceptions and definitions of wife abuse help determine the research techniques used to study this problem (Ellis, 1987a). In the discussion that follows, we will review the extent of wife abuse as revealed by a variety of methods.

How Many Canadian Wives Are Abused?

A major problem confronting researchers is eliciting accurate wife abuse data. No matter what research technique is employed, sociologists cannot avoid the problem of under-reporting. Many women will not communicate their victimization to doctors, social workers, police, family, friends, researchers, and others because of embarrassment and shame, fear of reprisal by their partners, memory error, or they may perceive some abusive acts as too trivial or inconsequential to mention (Kennedy and Dutton, 1989; Smith, 1987; Okun, 1986; Dobash and Dobash, 1979). Furthermore, many "helping professionals" (Dobash and Dobash, 1979) infrequently record incidents of wife abuse that are reported to them (Currie and MacLean, in press; Okun, 1986). For example, when many doctors and hospital workers treat abused wives' cuts, broken bones and other injuries, they disregard the sources of these injuries (Stark et al., 1979). Other medical professionals recognize the causes but prefer to record them as "accidents" or "of unknown origin" (Dobash and Dobash, 1979).[8]

If medical records are problematic, the same thing can be said about police data. Historically, many police officers responded to wife beatings by classifying them as "domestic disturbances," "family problems," "homicides," and "assaults" (Okun, 1986). Since victim-offender relationships were not correctly documented, police documents mystify the true nature of abuse in conjugal settings (Edwards, 1989; Okun, 1986). Two key sources of this problem are an officer's individual experiences and

[8] Like many medical professionals, some social workers do not identify battered women as victims of male violence (Dobash and Dobash, 1979).

beliefs, and his or her professional socialization. Many police officers are, for example, reluctant to define a husband's violent behaviour as wife abuse because they also physically and psychologically victimize their wives and cohabiters. They are also influenced by a male-dominated subculture that espouses patriarchal values conducive to woman abuse (Dobash and Dobash, 1979; Ellis, in press; Edwards, 1989).

In sharp contrast to helping professionals who deliberately underreport wife abuse, many transition house workers attempt to provide as much information as possible. Two widely-cited, albeit methodologically problematic, Canadian studies conducted by MacLeod (1980, 1987) report incidence rates derived mainly from women's shelters. Based on the statistics gathered in her first inquiry[9], MacLeod (1980: 1) asserts that " ... every year, 1 in 10 Canadian women who are married or in a relationship with a live-in lover are battered." In her second report, she (1987) maintains that at least one million, or one in eight women, were abused by their male partners in 1985.[10]

With the help of shelter staff, MacLeod was able to significantly increase public awareness of wife abuse in Canada (Smith, 1987). Nevertheless, her studies are not methodologically sound and thus do not provide reliable incidence rates of wife abuse (Ellis, 1987a). According to Smith (1989a), the above estimates are slightly better than guesses because of three major pitfalls. First, shelter residents are not representative of the entire Canadian female population. Second, some of the women included in the divorce data obtained in MacLeod's first study probably also stayed in transition houses. Thus, they were counted twice. Third, conclusions based on a combination of divorce and transition house data are highly suspect.

In sum, shelter staff and other helping professionals, such as lawyers, women's groups, and other social service personnel, are unreliable sources of national and regional data on the incidence and prevalence of wife abuse.[11] These people can only provide important information on individuals who are officially designated as victims. Despite their

---

[9] The conclusions presented in this report are also based on information derived from women who petitioned for divorce because of physical cruelty in 1978.

[10] The methodology used in MacLeod's (1987) study is superior to the techniques employed in her first investigation. Since her second study has been well documented and critiqued elsewhere, it will not be given much attention here.

[11] Incidence refers to the number of women who report being victimized during the past year. Prevalence is the percentage of women who report ever having been abused (Smith, 1987).

shortcomings, only representative sample surveys can advance our knowledge of how many wives are victimized in the population at large (Smith, 1987). Prior to examining the survey literature, we will present official data on a form of wife abuse that is not addressed in both self-report and victimization surveys—homicide. Unlike other types of government crime data, murder statistics are generally reliable because "dead bodies are almost always reported" (Boyd, 1988: 54). Furthermore, most murderers reveal their crimes to the police and do not avoid detection (Boyd, 1988). Thus, there is no significant "dark figure" of murder (Taylor, 1983).[12]

Homicide

Canadian women are more likely to be killed by unsafe working conditions created by their employers than by individuals outside the workplace (Reasons et al., 1981), an issue which will receive considerable attention in Chapter 5. While occupationally-related violence is a major social problem in this country, many women worry more about being victims of interpersonal homicide. Moreover, even though they are abused by their partners, a large number of females are more frightened of violence outside the domestic arena (Russell, 1982). Women's fear of male violence in any context is "well-founded" (Hanmer and Saunders, 1984); however, most homicide victims are related to their assailants.

In Canada, the legal term homicide includes three categories: murder, manslaughter and infanticide (Johnson, 1990). Most (39%) of the Canadian homicides solved by the police between 1974 and 1987 were classified as domestic homicides, and men who killed their wives or cohabiting partners were the largest cohort of perpetrators (37%). Most of the legally married offenders used guns to kill their wives (50%); however, common-law husbands used guns (34%) and beatings (30%) in roughly equal proportions (Johnson and Chisholm, 1990). Therefore, contrary to popular belief, Canadian women are more likely to be killed by their husbands than by strangers in the street (Johnson, 1990). The major motives for these fatal attacks are anger, jealousy, revenge and quarrels (Daly and Wilson, 1988; Boyd, 1988).

Official murder data are reliable, but statistics such as the Canadian Uniform Crime Reports (CUCR) provide inaccurate accounts of: (1) the

---

[12] Police statistics, however, do not include both missing persons who were murdered and murders disguised as accidental deaths or suicides (Koenig, 1987).

extent, distribution, and impact of interpersonal crimes and (2) the public's perceptions of and experiences with the criminal justice system (Solicitor General of Canada, 1983). In response to these and other criticisms of official statistics,[13] the Ministry of the Solicitor General of Canada, with the help of Statistics Canada conducted the Canadian Urban Victimization Survey (CUVS) in 1982, and Statistics Canada administered the General Social Survey in 1988.

These state-directed studies have made a significant contribution to Canadian victimology. Like all victimization surveys, they show that many crimes are not reported to the police (Solicitor General of Canada, 1983). Nevertheless, these surveys have major shortcomings that preclude an adequate sociological understanding of wife abuse. It is to these studies that we now turn.

Canadian Urban Victimization Survey (CUVS)

The CUVS was created because of a dissatisfaction with official crime data and a greater concern for crime victims within both the academy and the state (Walklate, 1989; DeKeseredy and Maclean, 1991). With regard to the first issue, police statistics cannot yield accurate estimates of the incidence and prevalence of wife abuse. Many acts are not revealed to the police for some of the reasons described previously (e.g., shame, fear of reprisal, etc.). CUCR data are also occasionally inflated or deflated by police officials " ... intent on proving some point through the manipulation of statistics" (Karmen, 1990: 52).

Another major pitfall of official data is that, except for cases of homicide and motor vehicle theft, they provide poor information on crime victims (Solicitor General of Canada, 1986; Evans and Himelfarb, 1987).[14] Similarly, before the late 1960s, the major thrust of criminological research was characterized as "offenderology" in which the main focal point of research was the offender (Karmen, 1990). Victims were given

---

[13] For a more comprehensive critique of Canadian official data, see Evans and Himelfarb (1987) and MacLean (1986).

[14] The CUCR procedure is being modified to include more data on victims (DeSilva and Silverman, 1985).

attention only if they could offer researchers information on perpetrators (Pointing and Maguire, 1988). A combination of social scientific and political developments occurred in the last three decades that shifted the emphasis from offenders to victims.[15] Many government officials and scholars now realize that victimization research is vital for capturing reliable crime data that can lead to the development of useful policies (DeKeseredy and MacLean, 1990).

In summary, the CUVS is the product of both the development of victimology as a major subdiscipline of criminology and practical Canadian criminal justice policy concerns (DeKeseredy and MacLean, 1991). Since the methods used in the CUVS are well documented elsewhere (Catlin and Murray, 1979; Evans and Leger, 1979; Solicitor General of Canada, 1983, 1984a, 1984b, 1985a, 1985b, 1985c, 1986, 1988), only a summary will be provided here.

The Ministry of the Solicitor General of Canada, with the assistance of Statistics Canada, conducted the CUVS in 1982. A representative sample of more than 61,000 household residents, 16 years of age or older, were interviewed by telephone in seven cities: Greater Vancouver, Edmonton, Winnipeg, Toronto, Montreal, Halifax-Dartmouth, and St. John's. The major objectives of this study were to acquire information on the frequency and distribution of reported and unreported crimes that occurred between January 1 and December 31, 1981, the impact of victimization, public perceptions of both crime and the criminal justice system, and public knowledge of, and involvement in crime compensation and crime prevention programs (Solicitor General of Canada, 1983).

The CUVS obtained little information on wife abuse because it was not designed specifically to gather data on this problem (Solicitor General of Canada, 1985a). The CUVS was presented to subjects as a crime study. A salient limitation of using a "crime survey" to obtain wife abuse data is that many victims do not perceive their partners' violent actions as crimes in the legal sense (Straus, 1989).

Another problem with employing the CUVS to investigate wife assault is that subjects were not asked directly if their husbands or ex-husbands had attacked them. Rather, they were asked to report whether they were attacked, and what their relationship to the perpetrator was. According to Smith (1987: 177), "This made it easy for those victims who were so

---

[15] Examples of these developments are the growth of victimology, the civil disturbances of the 1960s, "law and order" campaigns of right wing governments, and both the human rights and feminist movements (Elias, 1986; Karmen, 1990; Mayhew and Hough, 1988).

inclined to avoid the subject of marital violence altogether." Furthermore, no reliable distinctions between attacks that took place while victims were married and those that occurred after separation can be made (Dutton, 1988).

The CUVS has also been criticized for ignoring a wide range of psychological assaults. Only "face-to-face verbal threats" are investigated (Solicitor General of Canada, 1985a). This is a major pitfall because many women are targets of either verbal or symbolic aggression (DeKeseredy, 1988b; DeKeseredy and MacLean, 1990; MacLeod, 1987). By ignoring this conduct, the CUVS implicitly assumes that physical violence is more serious or painful than emotional maltreatment (DeKeseredy and MacLean, 1991). Many victims and shelter workers strongly disagree with this assumption (MacLeod, 1987).

The CUVS did not measure the incidence of wife abuse among rural, homeless, and minority women. Many poor females were also excluded from the sample. Rural data are not reported because the survey was restricted to urban centres. The high cost of studying crime in rural areas (MacLeod, 1987) probably influenced the Ministry of the Solicitor General to avoid them. Nevertheless, many women are victimized in rural areas (Lupri, 1990; MacLeod, 1987; Sharp, 1990). Furthermore, research shows that woman abuse may be more prevalent in rural communities than in cities or large towns (LaPrairie, 1983).

The dearth of information on both homeless and many low-income women is the result of random digit dialling (RDD) telephone interviewing procedures (Smith, 1989b). Women coerced to live on the streets cannot be contacted by telephone. These people should be included in any sampling design because many of them were assaulted by their male partners (Bard, 1988; DeKeseredy and MacLean, 1991; Barak, 1991). Harman (1989) found that after leaving their violent partners, many women could not acquire adequate financial and housing support from the state, families, and friends. Their only option was to either live on the streets or reside temporarily in shelters.

Many women are "homeful" (Harmen, 1989) but they cannot afford telephones. The exclusion of these people leads to a conservative bias in the estimate of wife abuse (DeKeseredy and MacLean, 1991). A large number of wives are abused in low income families (Kennedy and Dutton, 1989; Lupri, 1990; Smith, 1985, 1990a), and as Smith (1989b: 309) points out, "The negative relationship between income and abuse compounds the low-income bias among households without telephones."[16]

The CUVS has also been criticized for incorrectly portraying all female respondents as members of a homogeneous group (DeKeseredy and MacLean, 1991). Differences in the extent and form of abuse among distinct class and ethnic categories are not examined despite the fact that differences between people in diverse sub-groups do exist (Jones et al., 1986; Schulman, 1979: Straus et al., 1981). In Canada, for example, Native women are at greater risk of being battered and sexually assaulted than are white, middle class women (MacLeod, 1987). The key determinants of this variation are low socio-economic status, isolation, and vulnerability to other problems, such as social dissolution and alcohol abuse.

The CUVS yields findings that greatly underestimate the amount of wife abuse in Canada. Excluding threats with no physical attacks, the incidence rate is very low—less than one percent (Research and Statistics Group, 1984). Like the CUVS, cycle three of General Social Survey does not provide a reliable estimate of the amount of wife abuse in Canada.

The General Social Survey (GSS)

The third cycle of the General Social Survey (GSS), conducted in January and February 1988 by Statistics Canada, was a telephone survey which gathered accident and criminal victimization data from 9,870 persons 15 years of age and older in ten provinces. One of the principal objectives of this study was to gather information on the following issues: knowledge of victim services, perceived risk of accidental and criminal victimization, and kind and number of times respondents had been involved in accidents and crimes during 1987 (Sacco and Johnson, 1990).

Like the CUVS, the criminal victimization component of the GSS focused on incidents officially designated as criminal. It was not designed specifically to investigate the extent and nature of wife abuse. Although the GSS was modeled after the CUVS, there are three major differences between the two studies. The first and most obvious distinction is that the GSS was a national study which included both urban and rural subjects. The CUVS, as stated previously, used a limited sampling frame—seven metropolitan areas (Statistics Canada, 1990).

---

[16] Smith also contends that random digit dialling telephone coverage is "so good" that this limitation is not a major problem.

Second, unlike the questionnaire used in the CUVS, the GSS instrument was designed to encourage respondents to recount attacks by family members. According to Statistics Canada (1990: 2):

> In order to identify victims of assault, respondents to the CUVS were asked if, in the previous year, they had been attacked or threatened with an attack in any way. Respondents to the GSS were asked the same question, but with the reminder that an attacker could be anyone at all, including members of the respondent's own household.

The third dissimilarity is that multiple crimes against the same victim are counted differently in the two studies. A "series" event was operationalized as five or more acts in the CUVS and as three or more in the GSS. Respondents were asked to report on the most recent incident in the series with this act being considered as representative of all incidents. "When estimates were made for the general population, a series of incidents was counted as a single incident in the CUVS and as three separate incidents in the GSS" (Statistics Canada, 1990: 2).

Some of the criticisms of the CUVS described earlier can also be directed at the GSS. Given these limitations, it is no surprise that the findings provide an inadequate account of the amount of husband-to-wife abuse in the Canadian context.

Sacco's and Johnson's (1990) report, *Patterns of Criminal Victimization in Canada*, does not include a comprehensive analysis of the relationship between offenders and victims. For example, variations in abuse across marital status categories are not presented. However, Johnson (1990) provides some relevant GSS data. She refers to wife assault as "assaults or sexual assaults against a female victim by her spouse or ex-spouse" (1990: 169). Assault ranges from face-to-face verbal threats to assaults with major injuries, and sexual assault refers to rape, attempted rape and molesting (Statistics Canada, 1990). The incidence rate presented in this report is low—1.5 percent or approximately 1,500 per 100,000 women. Johnson (1990) states that this figure should be used with caution because it has high sampling variability

In summary, since both the CUVS and the GSS were not designed specifically to study violence against women in intimate, heterosexual relationships, they do not provide a comprehensive sociological understanding of wife abuse. Canadian representative sample surveys that used the Conflict Tactics Scale (CTS) (Straus, 1979) provide more accurate estimates than government inquiries because they were devised to do so. Nevertheless, the CTS also has numerous shortcomings that are made explicit in the discussion that follows.

Conflict Tactics Scale Surveys (CTS)

The most common measure of non-sexual violence against women in both Canada and the U.S. is the CTS (Straus, 1990). It is a quantitative measure that consists of 18 items and measures three different ways of handling interpersonal conflict in intimate relationships: reasoning, verbal aggression[17] and physical violence. The items are categorized on a continuum from least to most severe with the first ten describing non-violent tactics and the last eight describing violent strategies.[18] The last five items, from kicked, bit or "hit with a fist" to "used a knife or a gun" make up the severe violence scale.

The CTS used to measure wife abuse[19] is generally introduced as follows (Straus et al., 1981: 256):

> No matter how well a couple gets along, there are times when they disagree on major decisions, get annoyed about something the other person does, or just have spats or fights because they're in a bad mood or tired or for some other reasons. They also use different ways of trying to settle their differences. I'm going to read a list of some things that you and your (wife/partner) might have done when you had a dispute, and would first like you to tell me for each one how often you did it in the past year.

Table 2-1[20] presents incidence and prevalence rates of abuse reported in national (Lupri, 1990) provincial (Kennedy and Dutton, 1989), and city-wide Canadian studies (Brinkerhoff and Lupri, 1988; Smith, 1985, 1987). The physical violence figures are significantly higher than those obtained by the CUVS and the GSS. Thus, for the purpose of studying male-to-female violence in conjugal settings, the CTS is a valid and reliable alternative to the methods employed in government crime surveys.[21]

---

[17] DeKeseredy (1988b, 1989a) and Hornung et al. (1981) refer to the verbal aggression items as psychological abuse measures.

[18] Smith (1987, 1989a, 1990) modified the CTS by including an additional item.

[19] The CTS can also be used to measure child abuse and both physical and psychological assaults against parents, dating partners, and siblings (see Straus et al., 1981; Straus and Gelles, 1986; Straus and Gelles, 1990; Pirog-Good and Stets, 1989; DeKeseredy, 1988b).

[20] This is a modified version of a table of woman abuse surveys presented in Smith's (1989a) report.

[21] The CTS has high reliability, concurrent and construct validity (Straus et al., 1981).

TABLE 2-1: Wife Abuse Surveys

| Survey | DESCRIPTION OF SURVEYS | | | | ABUSE RATES | | | |
	Survey location and date	Sample description	Interview mode	Measure of abuse	Abuse past year	Severe abuse past year	Abuse ever	Severe abuse ever
Brinkerhoff & Lupri (1988)	Calgary 1981	562 men and Women	Face-to-face & self-administered questionnaire	CTS (men only)[a]	24.5%	10.8%	....	....
Kennedy & Dutton (1989)	Alberta 1987	1,045 men and women	Face-to-face & phone	CTS (aggregate)	11.2%	2.3%	....	....
Lupri (1990)	Canada National 1986	1530 married or cohabiting men and women	Face-to-face & mail questionnaire	CTS (men only)	17.8%	10.1%	....	....
Smith (1985)	Toronto 1985	315 women aged 18-25	Phone	CTS/open questions and 1 supplementary question	10.8%	....	18.1%	7.3%
Smith (1987)	Toronto 1987	604 presently or formerly married or cohabiting women	Phone	CTS and three supplementary questions	14.4%[b]	5.1%	36.4%[c]	11.3%

[a] men-as-aggressors.
[b] past year rates based on the CTS alone.
[c] abuse ever rates based on CTS (25.0, 7.8) plus supplementary questions.

It should be noted that some of the studies described in Table 2-1 include separated and divorced subjects (Kennedy and Dutton, 1989; Smith, 1985, 1987; Lupri, 1990). These people have the greatest risk of being victims or perpetrators of violence, an issue that will be given considerable attention in Chapter 3.

Many critics, especially feminists, assert that CTS data misrepresent the social reality of wife abuse and other forms of female victimization (e.g., premarital woman abuse) (Dobash and Dobash, 1988; Breines and Gordon, 1983; DeKeseredy and MacLean, 1990). Others argue that CTS findings have the potential to be used to obstruct efforts to provide adequate state support for abused women (DeKeseredy, 1988a). These criticisms warrant attention here.

Criticisms of the CTS[22]

Since the CTS categorizes abuse on a continuum from least to most severe, it assumes that physical assaults are worse than psychological abuse (Breines and Gordon, 1983). Many women, however, disagree with this conception. For example, as was discussed previously, Walker (1979) found that most of her subjects regarded incidents of psychological humiliation and verbal harassment as their worst experiences.

Related to the limitation of rank-ordering behaviours in a linear fashion is the assumption that the three items that constitute the "minor violence" subscale (e.g., threw something at her, pushed grabbed or shoved her, and slapping) are less injurious than those included in the "severe violence" subscale (DeKeseredy and MacLean, 1990). If a woman indicates that her partner slapped her, this incident is generally labelled as minor; however, a slap can break teeth or draw blood (Dobash and Dobash, 1988; Smith, 1987).[23] Thus, it should be coded as an act of severe violence.

Smith (1987) is the only Canadian researcher to have responded to this criticism. In addition to using the CTS, Smith asked supplementary open- and closed-ended questions. Consequently, four minor violence disclosures were recorded as severe " ... on the basis of the victim's in-depth account of the incident and its aftermath, such as whether she

---

[22] For a response to various criticisms of the CTS, see Straus (1990).

[23] One of Smith's (1986) respondents received a slap that loosened a few of her teeth.

sustained an injury, required medical assistance, or needed to call the police (1987: 181)."

The CTS misses many forms of abuse such as scratching, burning, suffocating, squeezing, and sexual assaults[24] (Smith, 1986). Nevertheless, Smith (1987) shows that supplementary questions can elicit data on these behaviours. For example, his second supplementary question produced 67 reports (11 percent of the total sample) of sexual abuse. Twenty of these respondents denied ever being assaulted in response to earlier questions.

The CTS was designed to measure only the incidence of both violent and psychologically abusive acts. Thus, it ignores the context and motives of violence in marital relationships. This limitation warrants considerable attention here because both Canadian (Brinkerhoff and Lupri, 1988) and U.S. sociologists (Straus, 1989; Straus et al., 1981; Straus and Gelles, 1986; Stets and Straus, 1990) present CTS-based data which show that women use violence about as often as men. These findings have been used to support the contention that many men experience "husband abuse" (McNeely and Robinson-Simpson, 1987; Steinmentz, 1977–78; Straus, 1989; Stets and Straus, 1990). However, in our earlier discussion on gender-neutral definitions, we showed that women's violence is primarily in self-defence. Furthermore, the fact that many men underreport abuse (Smith, 1987; Browne, 1987) challenges the mutuality of violence assertion (DeKeseredy and MacLean, 1990). The misleading "mutual combat" (Berk et al., 1983) data provided by Canadian researchers Brinkerhoff and Lupri (1988) can, like gender-neutral definitions critiqued earlier, enable patriarchal politicians to argue that since wives are as violent as husbands, new transition houses are not essential and existing shelters do not require expansion or refurbishing (DeKeseredy, 1988a; DeKeseredy and MacLean, 1990).

Brinkerhoff and Lupri are aware of the shortcomings of their research and they state that caution should be used when interpreting their results which show that except for "minor" types of violence, the reported amount of abusive acts committed by women against their partners is higher than the rates disclosed by men. They also maintain that women are more likely to sustain greater injuries than men, male violence causes more physical harm than female abuse, and women are at greater risk for being victimized in the home.

---

[24] U.S. dating violence researchers, Sigelman et al. (1984), revised the CTS by adding two measures of sexual aggression.

Although these arguments are valid, Brinkerhoff and Lupri do not support them with empirical data. Thus, according to DeKeseredy and MacLean (1990: 21):

> ... there is the potential for such research to be exploited by apologists for male violence. Without the context of the woman's assaultive behaviour, the argument that women are just as violent as men, assumes that women and men assault each other for the same reasons and creates the impression that the violence is gender-neutral.

Another major problem with the CTS is that it situates abuse items only in the context of settling quarrels or disputes in conflict situations. Many men beat their wives in order to "resolve" what they define as conflicts; however, many attacks "come out of the blue." Many women are beaten for no apparent reason, and some even attempt to avoid any type of confrontation with their husbands for fear of being abused (Browne, 1987).

Like quantitative measures in general, the CTS overlooks the wider social and ideological forces that influence men to harm their wives in order to maintain their dominance and control (Breines and Gordon, 1983; DeKeseredy, 1988a). Hence, CTS incidence and prevalence surveys lack a "sociological imagination" (Mills, 1959). These studies ignore the relationship between "personal troubles of milieu" and "public issues of social structure" (DeKeseredy and MacLean, 1990). According to Mills (1959: 8), the former are problems within an individual and his or her interactions within small groups. The latter are factors that transcend the narrow boundaries of a person's inner life and his or her microsociological relations with others.

Although the CTS suffers from a number of pitfalls, the representative sample survey data elicited by this measure are probably "the best available when it comes to estimating the incidence and prevalence of woman abuse in the population at large ..." (Smith, 1987: 177). Nevertheless, the CTS cannot provide data on "risk markers" (Hotaling and Sugarman, 1986) associated with wife abuse in the general Canadian population. A risk marker is any attribute of a couple, victim, or assailant that is associated with an increased probability of husband-to-wife abuse (Smith, 1990). It may or may not be a causal variable (Last, 1983). At least 97 potential risk markers have been identified in the U.S. literature (Hotaling and Sugarman, 1986); however, only the most salient sociodemographic factors discovered in Canadian research will be addressed in the next section on patterns of wife abuse.

Patterns of Wife Abuse

Survey research shows that wife abuse is endemic to many Canadian families. An explanation for the high incidence rates reported in the previous section is that "the marriage license is a hitting license" (Straus et al., 1981).[25] This thesis consists of two arguments. First, marriage is a unique relationship that places women at great risk for abuse. Second, married women are more likely to be beaten than unmarried women (Gelles, 1982). Many married women are at high risk for victimization, but abuse is not evenly and randomly distributed across all social groups (Smith, 1990; Walklate, 1989). Indeed, some women suffer more than others. Canadian studies reveal that wife abuse varies by income, education, age, marital status, employment status, religion, occupational status, and race/ethnicity.[26] The review below should be read cautiously because the present level of research makes it hard to categorize these nine variables as causes, co-occurrences, or consequences of wife abuse (Hotaling and Sugarman, 1986; Smith, 1990).

Income

Consistent with U.S. research (Straus et al., 1981), Canadian studies reveal an inverse relationship between income and wife abuse. Lupri's (1990) national study shows that low-income men were more likely to assault their wives than males belonging to higher income groups. Similarly, Kennedy and Dutton (1989) and Smith (1985, 1990) found that lower-income families are much more likely to experience husband-to-wife violence than their higher-income counterparts.[27]

Education

Two out four studies found a statistically significant association between education and abuse. In his Toronto study, Smith (1990) found an inverse relationship between husband's education and abuse. Consistent with this finding, data reported in Lupri's (1990) national survey reveal that among those aged 18–44, individuals who did not complete high school were more abusive than respondents with a graduate or professional degree. On the other hand, among subjects aged 45 years and

---

[25] This phrase was also presented in earlier studies (Straus, 1974, 1976; Gelles, 1974).

[26] For an excellent review of the survey research on sociodemographic factors associated with wife abuse in Canada and the U.S., see Smith (1990).

[27] See Smith (1989a) for a review of theories which are relevant to these results.

older, the highest violence rate discovered was for men with an incomplete university education. The Brinkerhoff and Lupri (1988) and Smith (1985) studies suggest that education is a poor predictor of wife abuse.

Age

The highest rates of abuse are found among young people. Kennedy and Dutton (1989) show that women aged 18–34 were six times more likely to be assaulted than females aged 45–64. In Lupri's (1990) national study, men aged 29 or younger were more likely to be perpetrators than older males. Similar results are reported by Brinkerhoff and Lupri (1988). Couples aged 30 or below had a violence rate three times higher than that among middle-aged and older couples. Smith's (1985, 1990) Toronto studies also show that young women are more likely to be victimized; however, his data are not statistically significant. According to Smith (1990), his results suggest a cohort effect.

Marital Status

Compared with married women, separated and divorced women are more likely to be abused by the men they live or lived intimately with (Kennedy and Dutton, 1989; Lupri, 1990; Smith, 1985, 1990). Cohabiting women are also more likely than married females to be assaulted by their partners (Smith, 1987; Ellis, 1989; Ellis and DeKeseredy, 1989; Kennedy and Dutton, 1989).

Employment Status

Lupri's (1990) national study reveals that unemployed men are more than twice as likely as both employed and part-time workers to abuse their wives. This finding was supported by Smith's (1990) survey. An inverse relationship between employment and abuse was also found by Smith (1985, 1990) and Kennedy and Dutton (1989); however, these data were not statistically significant.

Religion

This factor has received little attention in both the U.S. and Canada. The two Canadian city-wide studies that examined the relationship between religion and abuse did not uncover statistically significant associations (Smith, 1985, 1990).

Occupational Status

The influence of this risk marker has also received little attention in Canada. None of the three surveys that examined occupational variations in abuse report a significant association between assaults and husband's or wife's occupational status (Brinkerhoff and Lupri, 1988; Smith, 1985, 1990).

Race and Ethnicity

Of all the Canadian woman abuse surveys, only two studied ethnic and racial variations in abuse (Smith, 1985, 1990). No statistically significant differences across various ethnic groups were reported.

Summary

Although wife abuse is not uniformly distributed across the Canadian population, the most "consistent risk markers" (Hotaling and Sugarman, 1986) are youth, low income and divorce or separated status (Smith, 1990). Educational attainment, occupational status, and employment status are "inconsistent risk markers" (Hotaling and Sugarman, 1986) because the data pertaining to their influence are "mixed" (Smith, 1990). The influence of the other factors discussed in this section—religion, race and ethnicity—has not been given sufficient attention. Thus, according to Smith (1990: 45), " ... conclusions about these variables would be premature at present."

The identification of risk markers is necessary for the advancement of a sociological understanding of wife abuse in Canada. Theory construction and testing are equally important objectives. Attempts to address these two concerns are reviewed in the following section.

Theories of Wife Abuse

Canadian research on wife abuse is in its infancy, and thus, like U.S. research in the seventies, it is guided mainly by practical objectives (Gelles, 1980). For example, most of the survey work reviewed in this chapter was restricted to answering two important questions: (1) "how many wives are abused?" and (2) "what are the correlates of husband-to-wife abuse?" Although this work was guided by various theoretical perspectives, to the best of our knowledge there have been only two Canadian attempts to test sociological explanations of wife abuse. These studies were conducted in Toronto by Smith (1988, in press).

Smith's (1988) first attempt to test a theory addressed the debate concerning women's fear of violent crime. On one side of the debate is government sponsored research that states that women's fear of violent crime is subjectively based because it is significantly inconsistent with their chance of being victimized (Hindelang et al., 1978; Maxfield, 1984;

Solicitor General of Canada, 1985a). On the other side are feminist scholars who contend that women's fear of violent crime is objectively based because many females are victimized by male intimates, an issue that is not adequately examined by national crime surveys (Hamner and Saunders, 1984; Hanmer and Stanko, 1985; Stanko, 1987). Feminists contend that women's fear is a reflection of their actual violent experiences. Researchers such as Stanko (1988: 86) ask an important question: "Can women feel safe around male strangers when those familiar to them have violated their physical and sexual safety?"

Smith responded to this debate by arguing that the feminist perspective has not been "directly and systematically tested." Using data derived from his 1985 study, he tested and found partial support for the feminist position. Respondents who experienced severe forms of violence[28] were significantly more fearful than both women who experienced minor violence and those who were not victimized. Respondents who reported ever being abused by a male intimate, however, were not more afraid of being out alone at night than subjects who did not report being assaulted. In addition, the frequency and recency of abuse was not significantly related to fear.

Smith's (in press) second attempt at theory testing was also influenced by feminism. The principal objective of this inquiry was to "test the feminist hypothesis that wife beating results from adherence by battering husbands to an ideology of familial patriarchy" (in press: 2). Familial patriarchy refers to male power and control over women in the household (Ursel, 1986). Patriarchal ideology was defined in this study as:

> (1) a set of beliefs that legitimize male power and authority over women in marriage, or in a marriage-like arrangement, and (2) a set of attitudes or norms supportive of violence against wives who violate, or who are perceived as violating, the ideals of familial patriarchy (Smith, in press: 15).

Sexual fidelity, obedience, respect, loyalty, dependency, and sexual access are the key elements of this ideology that were examined in Smith's study.

Quantitative survey data gathered by telephone in Toronto support the feminist hypothesis. Based on interviews with female respondents, Smith concludes that husbands who adhere to an ideology of familial patriarchy are more likely to beat their wives than men who do not

---

[28] Severe violence was measured with CTS items n-r.

espouse patriarchal beliefs and attitudes. Smith's survey also shows that men with low incomes, low educational attainment, and low-status jobs are more likely than higher status husbands to adhere to the ideology of familial patriarchy.

If there is a dearth of theory testing in Canada, the same thing can be said about theory construction. So far, only Ellis and DeKeseredy (1989) and Ellis (1989) have built new theories of woman abuse that are relevant to this chapter. They have tried to explain why cohabiting, separated and divorced women are more likely than married women to be abused by the men they live with or have lived intimately with. Since these explanations are very complex, they will not be summarized here.

Some Canadian sociologists did not test or construct theories, but their research was driven by various theoretical approaches. For example, Brinkerhoff's and Lupri's (1988) Calgary survey was informed by both conflict (Sprey, 1979; Straus and Gelles, 1979) and social exchange perspectives (Blau, 1964; Gelles and Cornell, 1985; Nye, 1978; Safilios-Rothschild, 1976; Scanzoni, 1979). Furthermore, MacLeod (1987) discusses the relevance of what she refers to as "power-based" theories and learning explanations. Since these approaches have been adequately reviewed by Brinkerhoff and Lupri, and MacLeod, it is beyond the scope of this book to reproduce this information.

Policy Issues

What is to be done about wife abuse? As articulated in Chapter 1, there is a progressive answer to this question: female victimization in the marital context will be significantly reduced through a transformation to a socialist, feminist, anti-racist society (Schwartz and DeKeseredy, 1988; Messerschmidt, 1986). Since wife abuse is a major characteristic of patriarchal capitalism, this response appears to be valid; however, it is too simplistic (Walklate, 1989). Moreover, it is highly unlikely that a basic restructuring of the power relations between men and women will take place in Canada and the U.S. in near future. According to Messerschmidt (1986: 182), " ... nothing indicates the current existence, or early emergence of a unified socialist feminist revolutionary movement."

Another criticism of the above "idealistic" response is that for women who are presently being beaten on a regular basis, or who do not walk the streets alone for fear of being "mugged" or raped, revolutionary discourse has little to offer (Schwartz and DeKeseredy, 1991). Given these major problems, some sociologists, especially left realists (e.g., Lea and Young, 1984; Kinsey, Lea and Young, 1986), argue that the development of effective short-term policy proposals is important. Thus, the question that many contend we should be answering is "what to do while living under the current capitalist patriarchal system" (Schwartz and DeKeseredy, 1991).

We will critically evaluate some key attempts to answer this question. The strategies to be reviewed here can be categorized under the following headings: policing, economic policies, and social services. These initiatives are middle range policy alternatives that "do not compromise any overall design for fundamental social change ... " (Cohen, 1979). They may also help "chip away" at patriarchal capitalism (Messerschmidt, 1986).

Policing Wife Abuse

Until recently, Canadian police departments refused to take woman abuse seriously (Currie and MacLean, in press). Husband-to-wife assaults were not considered as important as violence against strangers on the street (Silberman, 1980). Some of the major reasons for this approach are respect for the "sanctity of marriage" and "privacy of the home" (Pahl, 1985); the view that wife abuse is marginal to the duties of "real" police work (Faragher, 1985); the perception that officers are at risk of physical injury (Ellis, 1987b); the belief that battered wives are legitimate victims (Dobash and Dobash, 1979); the reality that many police officers abuse their own wives (Ellis, in press); and police departments are male-dominated institutions that espouse a patriarchal ideology (Edwards, 1989; Snider, 1990).

Feminist efforts such as lobbying and education initiatives (Snider, 1990; Stanko, 1989; Currie, 1990), and empirical research (Sherman and Berk, 1984a, 1984b; Berk and Newton, 1985; Burris and Jaffe, 1983; Jaffe et al., 1986) have influenced police departments to take a more punitive approach to wife abusers.[29] Arrests are now much more common than they were before the 1980s (Jaffe et al., 1986; Ursel and Farough, 1986; Ursel, 1990). The influence of both the feminist movement and research findings on policing will be examined separately.

If Canadian police departments are institutions of capitalist male dominance, why would they respond positively to feminist groups' criticisms of their "minimal intervention" (Ellis, 1987b) approach to wife abuse?

---

[29] Canadian police officers have always had the authority to arrest and charge wife beaters (Currie and MacLean, in press).

Perhaps the transformation from "crisis intervention" to arresting wife abusers is the state's response to a "legitimation crisis" (Habermas, 1975). In his analysis of both Canadian and U.S. state policies on wife abuse, Ellis (1987b: 329) asserts that:

> Later, during the 1970s, when threats to the production of consensus by the state came from another politically significant constituency—women—the state's emphasis shifted from more benign "social worky" to harsher, law enforcement methods of intervening in domestic disturbances, especially wife abuse.

Thus, the "aggressive charging policies" directed by the Solicitor General of Canada in 1982 and by all provincial/territorial governments are not based primarily on a concern for women's safety (Currie and MacLean, in press). Rather, they are, to a certain extent, attempts to eliminate threats to dominant male interests (Barnsley, 1988). Feminist criticism, however, was not the only factor that prompted criminal justice personnel to adopt pro-arrest policies; experimental research also had a significant impact (Sherman and Cohn, 1989).

In Minneapolis, Sherman and Berk (1984a) examined the effects of three police responses to future incidents of misdemeanour wife assault: arrest, counselling and separation. They found that men who were arrested were less likely to abuse their wives during a six-month follow-up period than men who were counselled and separated from their wives for a brief period of time. Based on these data, Sherman and Berk conclude that arrest and incarceration alone will have a major deterrent effect.[30]

The above findings encouraged many police departments to formulate pro-arrest policies. According to Sherman and Cohn (1989: 117), "Over one-third of respondents from U.S. police departments in 117 cities said their policy had been influenced by the experiment ... " The research community reacted to the study by calling for further investigation (Dunford et al., 1990; Elliott, 1989; Lempert, 1989; Williams and Hawkins, 1989). In the U.S., the National Institute of Justice (1986) addressed this call by funding six replications of the experiment that were conducted in Omaha, Nebraska; Charlotte, North Carolina; Milwaukee, Wisconsin; and Colorado Springs, Colorado (Dunford et al., 1990). The last five are still in progress, and thus only the results from the Omaha inquiry will be presented here.

---

[30] In fairness to Sherman and Berk (1984a), they point out that their findings should be read with caution and that the data may not be generalizable to all U.S. cities. See Dutton (1988) for a more detailed critique of this experiment.

Sherman and Berk's (1984a) findings were not replicated in Dunford's et al.'s (1990) Omaha experiment. Arrest by itself did not deter men from abusing their wives more than separation or mediation. This evidence casts doubt on the deterrent power of mandatory arrest policies for minor acts of wife abuse. Dunford et al. (1990: 204) argue that "For those who are directly involved in responding to domestic assaults, it might be profitable to begin thinking about new or additional strategies for dealing with this problem." Like Sherman and Berk, however, Dunford et al. state that their conclusions should be read cautiously for three reasons.

First, the data from the other five replications have yet to be reported. Second, the data cannot be generalized beyond Omaha or beyond the kinds of incidents defined as eligible during the hours of the study. Third, even though Dunford et al. made a sincere attempt to replicate Sherman's and Berk's Minneapolis study, there are some major differences between the two experiments (e.g., variations in interview completion rates, differences in the areas of the cities included in the studies, etc.).

So far, no Canadian replications of Sherman's and Berk's study have been conducted. However, Jaffe et al. (1986) examined the long-term effects of police laying charges in cases of wife assault. Postcharge assaults were measured by counting the number of contacts abusers had with police in the following year, and by examining wives' reports of their husbands' violence[31] during the 12-month period after arrest. The victims' reports show, except for the use of weapons, a major reduction in all forms of violence during the year following arrest. For example, kicking, biting, or hitting with a fist declined from 57.2 to 22.9%.

Although there is empirical support for police intervention, some Canadian researchers ask "Is criminalization really a victory for women" (Currie and MacLean, in press)? Aggressive charging polices are not regarded as solutions to the problem of wife battery by some for the following reasons. First, since arrest polices are not implemented evenly across the country, many battered women are exempt from police protection. For example, in Toronto, black women are less likely to receive police assistance than white women (Lewis et al., 1989; Currie et al., 1990). Second, many victims do not want their husbands to be arrested because they believe that this response will terminate their marriages. Third, a "law and order" approach is seen as diverting attention away from the wider sociological forces that perpetuate and legitimate wife abuse (Currie and MacLean, in press; Snider, 1990).

---

[31] The CTS was used to measure violence.

The third criticism of police intervention is characteristic of a school of thought which Edwards (1989) refers to as "feminist idealism." Proponents of this approach generally argue that:

> ... the state and the law, the legal mechanism and the police, are part of a patriarchal structure, under which attempts at legal reform are only tinkerings within the overall system of control and regulation—so legal change serves only to perpetuate the basic conditions of patriarchy (Edwards, 1989: 15).

Like Canadian "feminist realist" Jane Ursel (1990), we disagree with the idealist position. Our interpretation of police research is that a criminal justice response can, to a certain extent, help battered women. However, criminal justice intervention is not the only strategy that should be used because it does not eliminate some major sources of wife abuse (MacLeod, 1987), such as economic inequality.

Economic Policies

Sociodemographic data reported previously (e.g., Smith, 1990) show that the highest rates of violence are found among lower socioeconomic groups. Policy proposals that target this problem are clearly necessary because a silent response to this association perpetuates a dominant tendency to " ... compartmentalize social problems along bureaucratic lines" (Currie, 1985: 18). For example, many people assume the criminal justice system is solely responsible for dealing with violent men and that other institutions should manage the social and economic problems that cause them to victimize their wives. Policy makers rarely consider how decisions on problems such as factory closures, reductions in welfare benefits and goods and services taxes may significantly affect the rate of wife abuse. According to Currie (1985: 19):

> The failure to make these necessary connections between causes and consequences stifles the development of intelligent policies to prevent criminal violence, and burdens the criminal justice system with the impossible job of picking up the pieces after broader social policies have done their damage.

Some policies proposed by progressive sociologists, especially U.S. left realists,[32] are sensitive to these concerns. Their contributions address the relationship between various forms of economic inequality and wife abuse. Michalowski's (1983) suggestions, for example, focus on the neg-

---

[32] For a comprehensive, critical examination of U.S. left realist criminology, see DeKeseredy and Schwartz (in press-b).

ative effects of unemployment and low wages. The following are examples of his strategies that are designed to be a financial responsibility for capitalists rather than the welfare state (1983: 14–18):

- Tax surcharges on industries attempting to close plants or permanently reduce a community's work force.
- Government laws demanding retraining and job placement for all workers displaced by new technology.
- A minimum wage level that is approximately 150% of the poverty level.

In contrast to the above initiatives, Currie's (1985, 1989) left realist agenda calls for both increased public and private support. He proposes a "social-environmental" or "human-ecological" approach that includes the following reforms:

- Increased wages for women.
- A wage policy similar to Scandinavia's "solidaristic" (Rehn, 1985) program.
- Publicly supported, community-oriented job creation.
- Improving the quality of work available to disadvantaged people.
- Intensive job training and supported work designed to help prepare both young and disabled people for stable careers.
- Paid work leaves.
- Job creation in local communities.

Messerschmidt's (1986) economic agenda is similar to those of Michalowski and Currie. His strategies, and the others set forth here, move beyond the limited boundaries of criminal justice reform (Gross, 1982; DeKeseredy and Schwartz, in press-b) to address wider economic forces which are major sources of wife abuse. These initiatives also avoid the pitfalls of compartmentalizing social problems along bureaucratic lines.

A few of the above proposals have been successfully implemented in other countries (Currie, 1985), and many sociologists contend that they would reduce the rates of predatory street crime and wife abuse in Canada and the U.S. (DeKeseredy and Schwartz, in press-b). Nevertheless, will Canadian politicians and voters respond favourably to left realist suggestions? At this point in time, probably not. According to Barak (1986: 201), left realist policies will not be developed and implemented by the state until " ... politicians, policy analysts, and the public are exorcised of current crime causation myths,[33] and not until many people

---

[33] For a more comprehensive analysis of crime myths, see Pepinsky and Jesilow (1984).

are ready to challenge some of our most inbred cultural and political assumptions." The exorcism that Barak is calling for will not be an easy task because major elements of the left realist proposals include eliminating the gains powerful Canadians have made under the current patriarchal capitalist order (DeKeseredy and Schwartz, in press-b).

Social Services

Expanded social services, such as short-term emergency shelter and housing assistance, are also required to curb female victimization in conjugal relationships (Messerschmidt, 1986). For example, many abused women stay with their partners because they are financially dependent and cannot survive without their spouses' economic support. This problem is more acute for unemployed women with children. With no refuge from violence and other forms of abusive conduct, many women have no choice but to remain in relationships that threaten their (and their children's) physical and psychological well-being (DeKeseredy, 1988a).

The number of Canadian battered women's shelters has tripled since 1979. While this is a positive reform, emergency shelters are generally overcrowded and many victims are reluctantly turned away (MacLeod, 1987).[34] Therefore, government funds should be used to open new shelters. Moreover, the state should give private citizens money to look after battered women who are denied access to emergency housing (Bowker, 1983).

Social support, through emergency shelters, is essential and must not be eliminated. But this assistance is not enough (Harman, 1989). In order to guarantee safety, autonomy, and self-reliance, state-subsidized housing must be provided. If victims are unable to afford a home or an apartment, they may return out of economic desperation to their violent husbands (Ellis, in press; Harman, 1989). On the other hand, they may become totally dependent on the shelter system that is a reflection of the wider patriarchal capitalist forces that perpetuate and legitimate woman abuse. For example, in her participant observation study of homeless women, Harman (1989: 106) reports that:

> The hostel has come to replace home for them. Women who become dependent upon hostels learn that there they may exist, in perpetuity, without money or resources of any kind. The hostels replace traditional female roles by being modeled after homes and requiring

---

[34] If a shelter has no vacancies, the staff attempt to place women in safe houses or provide other means of ensuring their safety (MacLeod, 1987).

women to do daily housekeeping chores, and by subjecting them to the rules and regulations of a larger structure that makes the decisions and has disciplinary power. In other words, they teach, foster, and reward domesticity.

Summary

The foregoing discussion critically reviewed sociological answers to six questions: (1) who is a wife?; (2) what is wife abuse?; (3) how many Canadian wives are abused?; (4) what are the patterns of wife abuse?; (5) what causes wife abuse?; and (6) how can we stop wife abuse?

The answer to the first question depends on whether researchers define cohabiters as marital rather than dating partners. For purposes of this book, a wife refers to any woman who is legally married or is sexually and emotionally linked to a male cohabiter. A four-part rationale for this definition was provided in this chapter.

Debates surrounding the second question focus primarily on three issues that incorporate both political and technical concerns. These are: (1) breadth of definitions (broad versus narrow); (2) objectivity versus subjectivity; and (3) terminology (gender-neutral versus gender-specific terms).

All sociologists have problems gleaning accurate data on the amount and sociodemographic correlates of wife abuse There is no method that is without shortcomings. For example, official statistics can provide fairly reliable information on murder; however, they offer inaccurate accounts of nonfatal abusive incidents. While representative sample surveys that have used the Conflict Tactics Scale (CTS) also have many limitations, they provide the most accurate estimates of the incidence and prevalence of nonsexual wife abuse in the population at large. These studies also show that female victimization in conjugal relationships is not distributed evenly across the Canadian population. The most consistent risk markers are youth, low income, and divorce or separation.

Compared to their attempts to document the extent and distribution of wife abuse, Canadian sociologists have paid little attention to the question of "What causes wife abuse?" Although most of the research has been informed by various theoretical perspectives, only a handful of studies have tested theories. These inquires were conducted in Toronto by York University sociologist Michael Smith.

Progressive responses to the question "What is to be done about wife abuse" call for both radical structural change and short-term initiatives. Middle-range strategies that can reduce the incidence of wife abuse were categorized under three headings: policing, economic policies and social services. These initiatives may also lower the rates of premarital woman abuse—a problem which will be addressed in the next chapter.

3

PREMARITAL WOMAN ABUSE

C hapter 2 shows that the abuse of women in marital relationships
is a major social problem in Canada. But the victimization of
females is not restricted to the conjugal domain. Many women
are assaulted by their boyfriends. However, compared to what we know
about wife abuse, we know relatively little about male violence and
other forms of mistreatment directed against women in dating relationships. The principal objective of this chapter is to review the limited
amount of Canadian information on this issue.

What Is a Dating Relationship?

Married and separated people date; however, for the purpose of this
book, dating relationships are defined as associations between unmarried males and females that address at least four needs. These are recreation, socialization, status achievement, and mate selection (Skipper and
Nass, 1966). Some relationships are considered "serious" because they
involve a high degree of commitment and intimacy. Others are defined
as casual because both partners seek a "good time" with no future commitment or obligation (Eshleman, 1978). Although cohabiters are not
included in this definition, for reasons described in the previous chapter,
some sociologists assert that these people should be viewed as dating
rather than as marital partners.

What Is Premarital Woman Abuse?

Debates surrounding this question have not been as intense as arguments about definitions of wife abuse. Thus, only two of three key
issues discussed in Chapter 2 are of central concern here: terminology
(gender-neutral versus gender-specific terms) and the breadth of definitions (broad versus narrow).

Terminology

Most U.S. researchers regard abuse in dating relationships as a joint problem of both partners. Therefore, they use gender-neutral definitions such as the following: "dating violence," "courtship abuse," "premarital violence," "courtship aggression," and "courtship violence."[1] These terms are just as problematic as gender-neutral definitions of wife abuse (e.g., marital violence and spousal assault). Since the limitations of definitions that portray men and women as equally violent have been made explicit in Chapter 2, they are not reproduced here.

Gender-neutral definitions are not common in the Canadian literature. Of the small amount of articles that have been published, most of which were written by Walter DeKeseredy, only two include gender-neutral terminology (BWSS; DeKeseredy, 1989b). The rest feature definitions such as: "woman abuse," "premarital woman abuse," "girlfriend abuse," and "girlfriend assault."[2]

The Breadth of Definitions

Canadian sociologists, unlike most of their U.S. counterparts, have not restricted their research to acts of physical violence. In fact, all of the empirical studies reviewed in this chapter focus on both physical and psychological abuse. Sexual assaults, however, have not been consistently included in Canadian definitions. Some of DeKeseredy's (1988c, 1989c) university sample studies, for example, exclude these behaviours.[3] In addition, many other types of abuse, such as economic cruelty, are omitted.

In sum, the Canadian sociology of premarital woman abuse is characterized by a relatively small number of definitions, most of which are, according to pro-feminist researchers, "politically correct." Our definition is broad in scope, objective, and clearly recognizes women as the principal victims of abuse in the context of dating. Throughout this

---

[1] For a comprehensive collection of U.S. articles that include gender-neutral definitions, see Pirog-Good and Stets (1989).

[2] The last two terms are found in Mercer's (1988) study.

[3] Technical rather than theoretical or political concerns prompted the deletion of sexual assaults. The items used to measure this problem yielded an insufficient number of cases to examine the relationships between variables.

chapter, premarital woman abuse refers to any intentional physical, sexual, or psychological assault on a woman by a boyfriend, lover, or casual date. The term physical assault incorporates a broad range of acts, from pushing and shoving to murder (Gelles and Straus, 1988). Psychological abuse includes insults or nasty remarks, doing or saying something to spite a female partner, and threatening to hit or throw something at her.[4] Sexual assault refers to situations where men use or threaten to use force (e.g., arm twisting, punching, holding her down, etc.) to try to make their dates engage in kissing, petting, and vaginal, oral, and anal intercourse when they didn't want to.[5] Most of the research techniques evaluated in the next section are influenced by our definition.

How Many Women Are Abused in Premarital Relationships?

Survey research shows that woman abuse in dating relationships is a significant problem in the U.S. (Makepeace, 1981, 1986; Laner and Thompson, 1982; Sigelman et al., 1984; Roscoe and Callahan, 1985; Koss et al., 1987; Pirog-Good and Stets, 1989). Until recently, there were no comparable Canadian inquiries. Sociologists concentrated primarily on violence against married and cohabiting women in Toronto and Alberta. There is some survey data on premarital woman abuse; however, we still lack accurate estimates of this problem. For example, no comprehensive, national official statistics are available.[6] Also absent are na-

---

[4] This is a modified version of Straus' (1979) operational definition of verbal aggression. Other behaviours, such as sulking and "stony silence" (Straus et al., 1989) are equally important; however, they are excluded here because there is a lack of Canadian empirical data on these problems.

[5] This definition of sexual assault is informed by Koss and Oros' (1982) Sexual Experiences Survey (SES).

[6] MacLeod's (1987) national study provides some pertinent national data. She maintains that there is a large number of teenaged women who are battered by their boyfriends. This contention is debateable because of her problematic methodology (see Chapter 2).

tional, provincial, and city-wide self-report and victimization surveys.[7] For the time being, we must rely mainly on DeKeseredy's survey data which were gathered from a nonprobability sample of university students.[8]

Of course, some relevant information could be obtained from helping professionals; however, given the major limitations of their data (see Chapter 2), these people cannot make an important contribution to the sociological understanding of premarital woman abuse. Even homicide statistics are problematic.

Homicide in Dating Relationships

Unfortunately, the Canadian federal government does not report the exact number of women who were murdered in dating situations. Instead, they record the amount of people killed by "acquaintances." Statistics Canada (1984) defines acquaintance homicide as " ... an aggregate category of four detailed suspect-victim categories: lovers' quarrels or love triangles, close acquaintances, casual acquaintances, and business relationships." In 1988, solved acquaintance killings accounted for approximately 42.6 percent of all homicides in Canada and 1.9 percent of these murders apparently took place in intimate relationships (Statistics Canada, 1990; Johnson, 1990).[9] Approximately 17 percent of the total number of acquaintance homicides were committed by "close" acquaintances (Statistics Canada, 1990). Since there is a lack of more precise published information on these killings, we can only speculate that a substantial portion of the victims were killed by their male dating partners.[10]

---

[7] There are, however, some relevant sub-national studies such as the CUVS (Solicitor General of Canada, 1985a) and Smith's (1987) Toronto inquiry.

[8] Women are also abused in high school dating relationships. Although this problem warrants much more attention from sociologists, social workers, criminal justice personnel, and society in general, it is not addressed here because there is very little research. Only one Canadian researcher, Sally Mercer (1988), gathered survey data on girlfriend abuse in secondary school relationships.

[9] According to Boyd (1988), the patterns of acquaintance murders are similar to those associated with domestic homicide. Acquaintance killers, however, are more involved in the use and distribution of illegal drugs, especially "hard drugs" like speed, heroine and cocaine.

[10] For example, Statistics Canada (1990) does not report the distribution of acquaintance homicide victims and suspects by gender.

Canadian surveys did not capture data on premarital homicides, but they provide information on non-lethal forms of abuse directed at women in university dating relationships. It is to these studies that we now turn.

The Extent of Woman Abuse in University Dating Relationships

To date, only one Canadian sociologist, Walter DeKeseredy, has conducted empirical research on woman abuse in university dating relationships. His main objective was to assess the potential contribution of social support theory to the sociological understanding of how male peers perpetuate and legitimate premarital woman abuse. While trying to achieve this goal, DeKeseredy (1988b, 1989a) also gathered the first Canadian exploratory data on the incidence of premarital woman abuse in a sample of male university students.

DeKeseredy's information came from self-report questionnaires[11] completed by a nonprobability sample of 308 male undergraduate students who attended 1987 Summer and Fall psychology, sociology, political science, natural science, and administrative studies classes at York University, University of Guelph, University of Toronto and McMaster University. Since the methods used in his research are described in detail elsewhere (1988b, 1989a), only a summary is provided here.

Woman abuse was defined as any intentional physical, sexual or psychological assault on a woman by a boyfriend, lover, male cohabiter or casual date. A slightly modified rendition of the 1986 version of the Conflict Tactics Scale (CTS) (Straus and Gelles, 1986) was used to measure physical and psychological abuse.[12] Only the introduction was revised for this study. For example, the word "dating" is absent from Straus and Gelles' preamble.

---

[11] Self-report surveys ask respondents to reveal information about their criminal and/or deviant activities. Most of these surveys have been administered in schools and have focused on juvenile delinquency (Hagan, 1985; Siegel, 1989).

[12] The CTS is the dominant measure of dating violence in the U.S. (Sugarman and Hotaling, 1989).

A psychological abuse index was constructed by combining three items: "insulted or swore at her; did or said something to spite her; and threatened to hit or throw something at her."[13] The last nine items, ranging from "threw an object at her" to "using a knife or a gun on her," constitute the overall violence index. An overall abuse index was created by combining the above 12 items. A subject was counted as having been abusive to his dating partner(s) if he engaged in one or more of the 12 acts during the year before the survey.

Since the CTS does not measure sexual abuse, the following two questions were used to operationalize this variable: [14]

Have you ever in the last 12 months:

1. Threatened to use physical force (e.g., twisting her arm, holding her down, etc.) to make a woman engage in sexual activities?

2. Used physical force (e.g., twisting her arm, holding her down, etc.) to make a woman engage in sexual activities.

The CTS data reveal that seventy percent (N = 214) of the respondents indicated that they had physically and/or psychologically abused their dating partners. Compared to most U.S. studies, this finding is very high and obviously due to the inclusion of responses to the three psychological abuse items (Laner, 1983).

The psychological abuse rate is only one percent lower than the overall abuse figure (69%) and the physical abuse rate is significantly smaller (12%, N = 36). Of those who physically assaulted their partners, 11 percent (N = 33) engaged in what some sociologists (e.g., Murray, Straus) refer to as "minor" types of violence (e.g., threw an object, pushing and slapping), and six percent (N = 18) stated that they committed one or more acts of severe violence (e.g., punching, kicking, etc.). Table 3-1 (DeKeseredy, 1989a: 58) shows that except for "used a knife or a gun," every type of abuse included in the CTS was reported by at least one subject although "minor" acts were reported more often. For example, the most frequently reported behaviours were insults or swearing, spiteful comments, and pushing, grabbing or shoving. Only 2.6 (N = 8)

---

[13] Hornung et al. (1981) argue that the third item is a form of both psychological and physical abuse. They also state that this act is a " ... transition point in the escalation of conflict from acts and language that are psychologically abusive to acts that involve physical aggression" (1981: 681–682).

[14] These measures are modified versions of questions found in Koss and Oros' (1982) Sexual Experiences Survey.

TABLE 3-1: Physical and Psychological Abuse

Types of Abuse	Percentage of Respondents	Number of Respondents
Psychological Abuse		
1. Insults or swearing	48.40	149
2. Spiteful comments	56.50	174
3. Threatened to hit or throw something at her	9.00	27
Minor Violence		
1. Threw something at her	3.00	9
2. Pushed, grabbed or shoved her	10.00	31
3. Slapping	5.00	15
Serious Violence		
1. Kicking, biting, hitting with fists	4.00	12
2. Hit or tried to hit with something	3.00	9
3. Beatings	1.30	4
4. Chokings	2.00	6
5. Threat with knife or gun	0.65	2
6 Used a knife or gun	0.00	0

percent of the respondents reported having sexually abused a dating partner(s) one or more times in the 12 months before the survey. The response frequencies for the two sexual abuse items are presented in Table 3-2 (DeKeseredy, 1988b: 56). These findings obviously reflect un-

TABLE 3-2: Incidence of Sexual Abuse

Type of Abuse	Percentage of Respondents	Number of Respondents
1. Threatened to use physical force to make a woman engage in sexual activities	1.3	4
2. Used physical force to make woman engage in sexual activities	2.3	7

derreporting because much higher rates of sexual assault were obtained in other studies.[15]

The above findings add to the growing body of research on the incidence of woman abuse in university dating relationships. Moreover, as was stated earlier, this survey was the first attempt to develop a Canadian data base. Despite these contributions, DeKeseredy's research suffers from a number of limitations; some of these were outlined in Chapter 2.

Criticisms of DeKeseredy's Research

Given the amount of attention devoted to criticizing the CTS in Chapter 2, for some readers (especially feminists), the most obvious pitfall is the use of this "empiricist" (Breines and Gordon, 1983) method. Nevertheless, the application of the CTS demonstrates a sensitivity to the shortcomings discussed previously. For example, since only self-report data from men were elicited, there was no attempt to support the "mutual combat" (Berk et al., 1983) image of dating violence. Furthermore, two questions were used to capture data on acts of sexual assault that are ignored by the CTS. Consistent with many other studies that employ the CTS, however, DeKeseredy's inquiry lacks data on many forms of

[15] Koss et al. (1987), for example, report that 25 percent of their male subjects indicated that they had engaged in sexual aggression since age 14.

abuse (e.g., burning, suffocating, scratching, etc.) Moreover, some violent acts may have been incorrectly coded.

Another limitation of DeKeseredy's study is endemic to all self-report surveys—memory error.[16] Some respondents forget some abusive acts, especially if they are considered minor (Smith, 1987). Others underreport attacks because of "backward telescoping." In other words, they remember abusive episodes as taking place later than the 12 month reference period. "Forward telescoping" may have also had an effect on DeKeseredy's study. Some respondents, for example, remember acts as occurring more recently than they really did (Smith, 1987).

The accuracy of DeKeseredy's data is suspect for two more reasons. First, some men remember abusive events, but they do not report them because of embarrassment, fear of reprisal, or the belief that they have nothing to gain by revealing their offenses (Kennedy and Dutton, 1989; Smith, 1987; Siegel, 1989). Second, some men choose not to report some acts because they regard them as too trivial or inconsequential to mention (Straus et al., 1981). These problems are unavoidable despite attempts to minimize underreporting, such as open- and closed-ended supplementary questions (Smith, 1987).

Additional questions minimize underreporting but they cannot eliminate the shortcomings of opportunity samples. They are unrepresentative and incidence rates cannot be generalized to a larger student population. Consistent with most U.S. dating violence studies (see Sugarman and Hotaling, 1989), a convenience sample was used in DeKeseredy's research. Although this technique is clearly problematic, a non-probability sample is appropriate for the objective of exploratory research. The next obvious step is to capture data from a representative sample of male university students—a procedure that gleans more accurate information.

DeKeseredy's sample, like those used in most self-report studies, only includes students (Hagan, 1985; Siegel, 1989; Sugarman and Hotaling, 1989). Thus, it excluded a substantial number of premarital woman abusers because many do not attend university or college. For example, in Bowker's (1983) sample of 136 battered women, only one out of five subjects obtained a four-year college degree, and their husbands were slightly less educated. Furthermore, 27 percent of the respondents were victimized during the dating period. Most of these people were abused only once or twice; however, five subjects were abused at least 14 times.

---

[16] This weakness is also characteristic of all victimization surveys, such as those discussed in Chapter 2.

In summary, DeKeseredy's methodology clearly suffers from a number of shortcomings. Nevertheless, his exploratory inquiry shows that woman abuse is a serious social problem in some southern Ontario universities. Moreover, the research:

> ... easily demonstrates that people will report crimes, that they will report crimes not known to officials, that they are highly likely to report those crimes known to officials,[17] and that their reports of crimes are internally consistent. These facts are rightly taken as evidence that the procedure is potentially useful as an alternative to traditional procedures (Hindelang et al., 1981: 212) ...

The CTS and sexual abuse data presented here offer no information about risk markers associated with woman abuse in university dating relationships. DeKeseredy, however, gathered some relevant information. In the next section, we will summarize his findings.

Patterns of Woman Abuse in University Dating Relationships

The sociological study of female victimization in university dating relationships is new and underdeveloped in both Canada and the U.S.; but there is considerably more U.S. information on risk markers.[18] This is not surprising given the handful of Canadian studies that are reviewed in this chapter. The dearth of information on the distribution of premarital woman abuse cannot only be attributed only to the small amount of research that has been conducted in this country. "Selective inattention" (Dexter, 1958) is also partially responsible. Many victimologists are not interested in premarital woman abuse and those that are have other theoretical and empirical objectives, such as those described in the previous section.

Until more data on risk markers become available, we have to rely on DeKeseredy's findings.[19] In contrast to research described in the last

---

[17] None of DeKeseredy's subjects were asked if their abusive conduct came to the attention of criminal justice officials.

[18] For a comprehensive review of this literature, see Sugarman and Hotaling (1989). They have divided risk markers into six categories: intrapsychic, personality, family history, interpersonal, stress, and sociodemographic.

[19] For more information on these findings, see DeKeseredy (1988b, 1988c, 1989c).

chapter, he did not find a relationship between woman abuse and the following sociodemographic variables: income, education, age, religion, occupational status,[20] and race and ethnicity. However, he discovered that victimization was significantly associated with dating status, stress, and social ties with abusive peers. It is to these relationships that we now turn.

Dating Status

Cohabiters are significantly more likely to have abused women than men who were involved in casual and serious dating relationships. This finding supports U.S. research (Cate et al., 1982; Henton et al., 1983; Laner, 1983; Laner and Thompson, 1982; Roscoe and Benaske, 1985)[21] and may be explained by the DAD model (Ellis and DeKeseredy, 1989). The DAD model contends that woman abuse varies with dependency, availability and deterrence. Dating status groups characterized by high dependency, high availability and low deterrence will generate a large number of woman abusers.[22]

According to Ellis and DeKeseredy (1989: 76) dependency refers to:

... a relationship between a person and another person, symbol, substance or material object characterized by physiological or psychological withdrawal pains contingent upon its unavailability and the absence of subjectively perceived alternatives.

Men in dating relationships characterized by a high degree of intimacy are more emotionally dependent on their partners than males in casual relationships. Highly dependent men are also more likely to use violence to establish or maintain the dependence or commitment of their girlfriends on them in contexts in which the interdependency symbolized by a marriage license is not available. Without a legal commitment, dependent men may abuse their partners to ensure that they will stay with them. Abuse is perceived as a way of increasing the level of emotional commitment among women (Billingham, 1987). Empirical support for this argument is found in the U.S. dating violence literature

---

[20] DeKeseredy did not examine the influence of this variable.

[21] The samples examined in these inquiries did not include cohabiters.

[22] This theory served as a "post-factum interpretation" (Rosenberg, 1968) because, for technical reasons, DeKeseredy could not use control variables to determine whether the relationship between dating status and woman abuse is affected or is impervious to other determinants.

(Makepeace, 1981; Cate et al., 1982; Henton et al., 1983; Roscoe and Benaske, 1985).

In addition to being emotionally dependent on female intimates, many woman abusers are dependent on drugs and alcohol. Moreover, Berk et al. state that "men with a history of problem drinking are more likely to inflict serious injuries" (1983: 302). Men who have lost their jobs or destroyed their marriages because of problem drinking, are over-represented among cohabiting men (Ellis and DeKeseredy, 1989). In sum, cohabiting men are more likely to be abusive than males in serious or casual relationships because they are highly dependent on their partners and on alcohol or drugs.

Obviously, in order to be victimized by a man, a woman must spend time with him. A woman who is most available to be abused is a person who spends the most time-at-risk (Cohen et al., 1981). Cohabiters report higher rates of abuse than men who belong to other dating status groups because they spend the greatest time-at-risk (Billingham, 1987; Laner and Thompson, 1982). Since they live with their partners, cohabiters have more opportunities to harm their partners than men who maintain separate residences.

Deterrence is an important variable for social control theorists. These scholars (e.g., Hirschi, 1969) are not interested in explaining deviant behaviour; rather, they attempt to explain variations in conformity to legal and social norms (Ellis, 1987a). Social control theory explains variations in conformity to criminal law and social norms proscribing pre-marital woman abuse by pointing to the losses that would be incurred if this conduct were discovered, publicized and punished. Men with the most to lose, with the greatest "stake in conformity" (Toby, 1957), are more likely to be deterred by the possibility of legal and/or social punishment. Those with the least to lose are least likely to be deterred by formal and informal sanctions.

Cohabiting men are more abusive than men involved in less serious relationships because they have a lower stake in conforming with social and legal norms proscribing woman abuse (Ellis and DeKeseredy, 1989). For example, since cohabiting men are more socially isolated in their communities (Stets and Straus, 1989), they are less concerned about loss of reputation as a punishment. Furthermore, many policemen offer co-habiting women little help because they are considered to be involved in immoral relationships. Female cohabiters may be viewed as not worthy of legal assistance (Yllo and Straus, 1981). Thus, male cohabiters are not likely to worry about criminal justice intervention.

Ellis and DeKeseredy (1989) argue that like men with a low stake in conformity, men with both a history of woman abuse and greater aggressive habit strength are overrepresented among cohabiting couples. Aggressive habit strength is a function of a person's past history of violence, and it is one the best predictors of future violence (Fagan et al., 1981; Monahan, 1981; Megargee, 1982). Other things being equal, the greater the man's aggressive habit strength, the less likely he is to be deterred by either formal or informal sanctions made contingent upon his violent behaviour.

In summary, Ellis and DeKeseredy's DAD model is a plausible explanation for the relationship between dating status and woman abuse. Nevertheless, until it is subjected to empirical evaluation, it is just a post-factum interpretation. Other theories could be equally plausible.

Dating Life Events Stress

A number of stress factors, such as academic workload, inadequate finances and job loss, are strongly related to premarital woman abuse in the U.S. (Makepeace, 1983, 1987; Sugarman and Hotaling, 1989). DeKeseredy, however, focused only on stress associated with male-female relationships. For the purpose of his research, stress refers to a dating life event that is " ... threatening or otherwise demanding and does not have an appropriate coping response" (Cohen and Wills, 1985: 312). A modified version of the College Students Life Events Scale (Levine and Perkins, 1980) was used to operationalize this variable. Respondents were asked to report how stressful the following six life events were form them in the 12 months before the survey: [23]

1. Girlfriend broke up the relationship.
2. Dates or girlfriends disapproved of your use of alcohol and/or drugs.
3. Experienced sexual rejection after you spent money on a date.
4. Dates or girlfriends won't have sex when you want.
5. You had to show your dates or girlfriends who was the boss.
6. Dates or girlfriends spent too much time with their female friends.

An index was constructed by adding participants' scores on each of the above items.

---

[23] The response categories were a great deal, considerable, moderate, little, and none.

DeKeseredy found that the more stress men experience, the more likely they will abuse their partners. However, for men who received informational support from the male friends,[24] the association is both weaker and statistically nonsignificant. On the other hand, the relationship between stress and woman abuse was stronger and statistically significant for men who dated women who used recreational drugs on dates (e.g., marijuana, hashish, etc.). This finding supports the rationale for using the drug variable as a control. Briefly, some men believe that recreational drug users are more likely than abstainers to engage in premarital sex. This notion is the result of information provided by male peer groups.[25] Of course, many female drug users abstain from sexual activities on dates. Nevertheless, if their partners' sexual expectations are not met, these men may experience stress which in turn leads to abuse.

Social Ties With Abusive Peers

Social ties with abusive peers (STAP) refers to bonds with male friends who physically, sexually and psychologically abused their dating partners or girlfriends. For respondents who experienced no or low amounts of dating life events stress, the relationship between STAP and abuse was not statistically significant. Moreover, a statistically nonsignificant association emerged when dating partners' use of drugs on dates was introduced as a control factor. Among high stress subjects, however, a stronger and statistically significant association was discovered.

Summary

Since there is a lack of data on sociodemographic risk markers associated with woman abuse in university dating relationships, we cannot make accurate statements about its distribution across the Canadian population. Moreover, the findings on the above correlates are suspect because they were gleaned from a convenience sample. Only representative sample surveys are capable of capturing reliable data (Smith, 1990). These studies would also enable researchers to rigorously test theories, such as the DAD model and the explanation for the relationship between stress and woman abuse.

---

[24] Informational support is guidance and advice that influence men to sexually, physically, and psychologically assault women.

[25] Women who drink heavily on dates are considered "legitimate sexual targets" (Kanin, 1985) because their high level of alcohol consumption is seen as an indication that they will engage in sexual intercourse (Berger et al., 1986; Kanin, 1984).

Theories of Woman Abuse in University Dating Relationships

According to Sugarman and Hotaling (1989: 28), "In some ways, dating violence research examines a phenomenon that is searching for a theory." Very little theoretical work is evident in the U.S. literature, and even less so in Canada. Instead, the major concerns of North American studies conducted to date are: (1) providing incidence and prevalence rates; (2) identifying correlates; and (3) "post hoc" explanations of data. The dearth of theorizing prompted DeKeseredy (1988b, 1988d) to construct and test the first Canadian theory of premarital woman abuse, one that integrates three distinct bodies of knowledge: woman abuse, social support, and reference others. He (1989c) also empirically assessed the buffering model's explanatory value.

Female victimization in university dating relationships is related to a variety of "support functions" (Cohen and Syme, 1985) provided by male peers.[26] The male peer support model was developed to explain this problem. This model is informed mainly by social support theory—a perspective that is generally used to explain how social integration, and the various resources provided by interpersonal relationships, determine people's ability to cope with stressful life events (Wills, 1985). Although social support theory deals mainly with health issues and not specifically with the relationship between male peer group dynamics and woman abuse, it is relevant to this problem.

For example, many male university students experience stress in dating relationships, such as arguments, sexual problems, and challenges to their patriarchal hegemony (Levine and Perkins, 1980). Some men attempt to deal with these problems themselves. Others turn to their male peers for social support. Social exchanges with male friends can encourage and legitimate female victimization (Bowker, 1983). Peer support can also relieve or prevent post-abuse stress by providing a "vocabulary of adjustment" (Kanin, 1967, 1985). In addition, male friends can influence men to mistreat their dates regardless of stress.

Male peer support is a central factor in the model presented in Figure 3–1.[27] This model explains how social interactions with male peers, and their nature, are associated with woman abuse. Figure 3–1 shows that

---

[26] For a comprehensive review of the sociological and social psychological research on this topic, see DeKeseredy (1990a).

[27] See DeKeseredy (1990b) and DeKeseredy and Kelly (1990) for a slightly revised version of this model.

FIGURE 3-1: Male Peer Suport Model

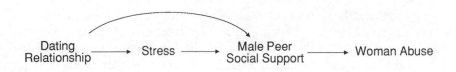

dating life events stress and social support influence the likelihood of abuse. Dating is related to stress and it motivates men to seek support from their male friends. Such support affects the probability of various types of victimization.

The model generated six hypotheses that were empirically tested. Since the results have been well documented in other publications,[28] they will not be reported in great detail here. Briefly, partial support for the model was found using data gathered from a sample described previously. However, several other factors, such as class, patriarchy, dating partners' drug use, and gender role socialization, need to be addressed in future attempts to revise the male peer support explanation.

DeKeseredy's other attempt at theory testing was also influenced by social support theory. A hypothesis derived from one variation of this perspective—the buffering model—was tested. Advocates of this theory assert that:

> ... support may intervene between the stressful event (or expectation of that event) and the stress experience by attenuating or preventing a stress response. In short, resources provided by others may redefine and reduce the potential for harm posed by a situation and/or bolster the ability to cope with imposed demands, hence preventing the appraisal of a situation as stressful (Cohen and Syme, 1985: 7).

---

[28] See DeKeseredy (1988b, 1990b) and DeKeseredy and Kelly (1990).

DeKeseredy argues that informational support buffers men from stress associated with premarital woman abuse. This hypothesis is based on research that shows that post-abuse stress[29] can be alleviated by male peers who provide abusers with justifications for mistreating dating partners. This discourse enables woman abusers to continue viewing themselves as "normal" and "respectable" males (Kanin, 1967, 1985).[30]

The quantitative survey data used to test the above male peer support model support his hypothesis. Guidance and advice conducive to the mistreatment of women appeared to have prevented abusive respondents from experiencing stress related to psychological and/or physical assaults. This conclusion, however, should be regarded with caution since a causal relationship was not clearly determined. Thus, the buffering hypothesis requires further testing. Again, the data are also suspect because they were gathered from a biased sample.

Policy Issues

For reasons articulated earlier in this book, middle range policy initiatives are necessary to curb premarital woman abuse. Idealistic discourse is of little value now. Some of the short-term initiatives discussed in Chapter 2 can reduce the number of women harmed in dating relationships; however, the strategies to be reviewed here either deal directly with the problem of female victimization in university dating relationships or are relevant to the data presented in previous sections of this chapter. These policies are categorized under three headings: (1) anti-sexist male collectives, (2) campus disciplinary proceedings, and (3) awareness programs. The first and third temporary solutions can also be applied in the struggle against wife abuse.

Anti-Sexist Male Collectives

Male peer support is a key correlate of both physical and psychological woman abuse in the context of post-secondary school dating. This is not surprising since "peer groups are an extremely important part of college students' lives" (Gwartney-Gibbs and Stockard, 1989: 200). University counsellors, campus "drop-in" centres, and university support

---

[29] Walker's (1977–78, 1983) research shows that some men display contriteness and beg for forgiveness after beating their wives. DeKeseredy (1988d) suggests that these behaviours are consequences of post-abuse stress.

[30] Symbolic Interactionist George Herbert Mead (1934) showed that an individual's mind and self is based on social exchanges with various people.

services for women should be sensitive to the leverage of male social networks in their efforts to end assaults on women. For both violent and psychologically abusive men who are influenced significantly by patriarchal or abuse-oriented peers, individualistic treatment and prevention initiatives are not likely to be effective. Instead, self-help groups modelled after Alcoholics Anonymous (AA) may be the most successful intervention technique for members of sexist subcultures of violence (Bowker, 1983).

Members of AA receive various types of support if they admit that they are alcoholics. They are also encouraged to interact with fellow members on a frequent basis, and to regularly contact members who are struggling to abstain from alcohol. AA offers problem drinkers " ... a new set of associations, the intensity, duration, frequency, and priority of which are intended to aid in the unlearning of conventional behaviour" (Pfhol, 1985: 259). AA can successfully stop people from drinking. Similarly, self-help groups can reduce premarital woman abuse (Adams, 1989).

University-based programs for men who abuse women should be modelled after anti-sexist male collectives like AMEND, RAVEN, EMERGE, New Directions, Vivre sans Violence (also known as Vi-Sa-Vi), and Entre-Hommes. Defined as profeminist, these agencies offer "hotlines" for men to call when they feel like assaulting their wives, girlfriends, or lovers (Finkelhor and Yllo, 1985). They also provide a peer group education that emphasizes that woman abuse is learned behaviour that is rooted in patriarchal social norms instead of being a function of individual or couple pathology (Adams, 1989). In addition to being informed by a feminist perspective, the above programs are influenced by social learning theory, the "men's movement," radical therapy, and political experiences (Adams, 1989; Schechter, 1982).

The principal objective of profeminist group sessions is to stop men from physically and sexually assaulting their partners. But even if clients do so, according to Quebec social worker Jurgen Dankwort (1988: 2):

... more subtle forms of abuse, such as emotional withholding, displays of anger, economic control or threats of infidelity will soon take the place of the physical attacks, if the underlying attitudes which give rise to abuse are not changed.

Therefore, anti-sexist collectives also encourage men not to use nonviolent methods of patriarchal control. Group sessions are contexts of anti-sexist education in which participants influence each other to eliminate all behaviours that undermine gender equality and their partners' individual freedom (Adams, 1989; Dankwort, 1988).

University support services for female students and employees, such as women's centres and sexual harassment centres, should help create and monitor profeminist programs for abusive male students. The assistance provided by these centres will guard against therapies that blame female victims (Dekeseredy, 1988b). Caution, however, is required for two reasons. First, some of the men who participate in profeminist self-help groups do so because their partners leave them and refuse to return until they do something about their violent conduct. Second, some men are ordered to participate in group sessions by various criminal justice personnel. Thus, for peer support to be successful, additional strategies, such as campus disciplinary proceedings, must be employed.

Campus Disciplinary Proceedings

University administrations are generally dominated by male decision makers. Some of these bureaucrats are either uncomfortable with or are uninterested in developing policies designed to reduce the number of women who are victimized by male students. In fact, some administrations and campus security officers have hidden reports of sexual assault (Schwartz, 1989). Since most universities rarely take punitive action against woman abusers, Schwartz (1989: 10) argues, "If college men feel they are above the law when they rape women, it is because they are. They are given virtually absolute protection from prosecution and punishment by the college community." Disciplinary procedures are thus clearly needed.

Perhaps some of the policy proposals suggested by U.S. researchers Ehrhart and Sandler (1985) are applicable to the Canadian context. Examples of their initiatives are (1985: 11):
- Immediate expulsion
- Suspension for a specified time
- Probation for a specified time
- Individual and group counselling
- Denial of campus housing
- Requiring the perpetrators to inform their parents
- Placing a letter in the offenders' permanent file
- Participation in community service, such as rape presentations
- A letter of apology to the victims

Several of these sanctions instead of only one should be implemented. They should also be administered regardless of the criminal justice system's response. Moreover, in order for these policies to be effective general and specific deterrents, and to send a message to all students that the university adminstration formally recognizes premarital woman abuse as deviant behaviour, they must not be kept confidential (Ehrhart and Sandler, 1985). Specific deterrence refers to the effects of punishment on offenders. General deterrence refers to the effects of an individual's punishment on a wider audience (Ellis, 1987a; Currie, 1985).

The peer support literature reviewed previously reveals that male social networks often encourage members to victimize their intimates. In particular, fraternities are "breeding grounds" for premarital woman abuse. They are also referred to as "rape cultures" in which the social exchanges between members are riddled with patriarchal attitudes (Schwartz, 1989). Ehrhart and Sandler (1985: 12) contend that fraternities that include individuals who sexually assault women should be subject to at least one of the following punishments[31]:

- Disbanding of the chapter
- Probation
- Loss of campus housing
- Suspending rushing for a specified time
- Prohibition of social activities for a specified time
- Prohibiting alcohol at fraternity events
- Prohibiting fraternity members from holding office in student government or having any campus position of leadership and status
- Prohibiting service projects for a specified period of time
- Requiring community service such as participation in rape prevention programs for all fraternity members
- Restricting female guests to the downstairs area of the fraternity during social events
- Requiring every fraternity to develop and record its official position on sexual violence and develop its own guidelines to ensure that the policy will be enforced

Sanctions such as those discussed here are, of course, necessary. Nevertheless, punitive measures do not adequately address the patriarchal attitudes and norms that perpetuate and legitimate woman abuse in university dating relationships (Currie and MacLean, in press). Awareness programs, however, can help universities deal with this problem. It is to these initiatives that we now turn.

---

[31] There is no reason why these sanctions could not also be administered to fraternities with members who physically assault (e.g., punch, kick, hit) dating partners.

Awareness Programs

While there are many methods of increasing student, faculty, support staff, and community awareness about premarital woman abuse, both researchers and practitioners are unclear about which strategies are the most effective (Schwartz, 1989). Nevertheless, there is a consensus about the need for campus discussion groups that address key issues such as gender role socialization, sexism in popular culture, rape myths, and sexual rights and responsibilities (Erhart and Sandler, 1985). Volunteers could coordinate group discussions; but, as Schwartz (1989: 13) points out:

> It is unreasonable to assume that even this single program could be run without at least enough money to hire a full time person to train and coordinate peer volunteers, to coordinate other campus wide efforts; and for extensive publicity and printing costs.

In addition to discussion groups, several other awareness strategies must be employed. Erhart and Sandler (1985: 14) provide a comprehensive list of programs for male and female students that could be developed and implemented at Canadian campuses. Rather than reproduce their entire agenda here, only a few salient examples are listed below:

- Student residence meetings that address "date rape" and other forms of woman abuse
- Freshmen orientation packets that include written materials on woman abuse
- Classroom presentations on sexism and male violence against women
- Workshops on gender roles
- Films on gender roles, the objectification of women, and violence

Summary

This chapter reviewed the limited Canadian sociological literature on an issue that warrants much more social scientific and political attention—premarital woman abuse. Since there is a dearth of information on the variety of ways in which women are mistreated in university dating relationships, debates surrounding some the key questions addressed here are not as lively as those discussed in Chapter 2.

The answer to the question "What is premarital woman abuse?" is contingent upon how sociologists define dating. In this chapter, dating relationships refer to associations between unmarried males and females

AUGUSTANA UNIVERSITY COLLEGE
LIBRARY

that address the following needs: recreation, socialization, status achievement, and mate selection.

In sharp contrast to most U.S. studies, gender-neutral terminology is not common in Canadian research. Moreover, the handful of definitions that have been developed in this country are broader in scope.

Since only exploratory survey data on the incidence of woman abuse in university dating relationships have been published, accurate estimates cannot be made. However, Walter DeKeseredy's research suggests that many men abuse their dating partners. Methodologically sound research is required to provide more support for this assertion. More information on the sociodemographic risk markers associated with premarital woman abuse is also necessary if we want to have an adequate understanding of its distribution.

If there is a shortage of information on the extent and distribution of premarital woman abuse, the same thing can be said about theory construction and testing. DeKeseredy responded to this problem by constructing and testing a male peer support model. He also tested one variant of social support theory—the buffering hypothesis.

A few temporary initiatives designed to reduce the number of women abused in dating relationships were discussed in this chapter. They were categorized under three headings: (1) anti-sexist male collectives, (2) campus disciplinary proceedings, and (3) awareness programs. These policies, like the strategies outlined in Chapter 2, may be effective in the struggle against rape and other types of sexual assault. These problems are addressed in the next chapter.

4

RAPE AND SEXUAL ASSAULT

There has been a great deal of public and academic debate during the last twenty years about what can be done to reduce the rates of rape and sexual assault. The debates have focused on a range of issues and problems, including assessing the amount of sexual violence, reasons why victims do not report their victimization, theories to explain why it happens, and various strategies to control it. This chapter reviews these and other issues with the objective of working toward a better understanding of social causes and control of sexual violence.

What Is Rape and Sexual Assault?

The rape/sexual assault literature offers an almost bewildering array of definitions. Debates on definitions have generally concentrated on such issues as gender-neutral versus gender-specific terms, and determination of the legal definition.

Two terms are of interest here: rape and sexual assault. The simplest definition of rape, defines it as an act of unconsented sexual intercourse forced on a woman by a man. Similarly, the simplest definition of sexual assault refers to unconsented sexual touching. Both definitions are problematic. Critics of the above definition of rape argue that it ignores the problem of homosexual rape. They maintain that all forms of sexual violence should be referred to as sexual assault (see, for example, Clark and Lewis (1977)) because this allows male and female victimization to be treated as equally serious events. It also shifts attention away from the sexual nature of the act, proving vaginal penetration, towards the violence involved. Other forms of sexual violence, they argue, are often as violent and sometimes more violent than some incidents of rape.

However, not everyone agrees that the term rape should be abandoned. Cohen and Backhouse (1980), as well as Hinch (in press), argue that abandonment of the term rape amounts to sweeping away its reality. The act of rape does not disappear by changing its name. Further, it can be argued that to be accused, charged and convicted of rape symbolically implies a more serious event than to be accused, charged and convicted of sexual assault. Even though some forms of sexual assault not involving penetration are more violent than some rapes, rapes are usually more violent than most non-penetration sexual assaults. Rape is a more violent event than is an incident in which a woman's breast or vagina is grabbed and the offender immediately runs away. To allow male and female victimization to be treated with similar seriousness, and to allow the more violent incidents of other types of sexual violence to be treated with more seriousness, it is not necessary to abandon the use of rape. Therefore, in this chapter, unless making reference to literature or laws which define it otherwise, rape refers to unconsented acts of penetration of the vagina, anus or mouth where these acts are intended for a sexual purpose. Sexual assault, unless referring to specific literature or laws which define it otherwise, refers to all other unconsented sexual touching not involving penetration.

The Legal Definition

Until 1983, the legal definition of rape in Canada was provided in Section 143 of the Criminal Code of Canada:

> A male person commits rape when he has sexual intercourse with a female person who is not his wife, a) without her consent, or b) with her consent if the consent (i) is extorted by threats or fear of bodily harm, (ii) is obtained by personating her husband, or (iii) is obtained by false and fraudulent representations as to the nature and quality of the act.

At that time, the law also specified a number of other sex offences, such as Indecent Assault on a Male, and Indecent Assault on a Female.

Critics argued the law not only treated male and female sexual victimization differently, it also contained unacceptable, anti-woman biases. For example, men could not be accused of raping their wives.[1] Further-

---

[1] While a married man could not be convicted for raping his wife, there were other charges which could have been laid against him. Husbands could have been charged with indecent assault, but this option was rarely used. The most frequent criminal charge laid against married men who raped or sexually assaulted in some other way their wives was common assault. This option, however, was not the usual practice. The usual practice was not to lay criminal charges of any kind. Occasionally, incidents in which married men raped their wives were used as evidence of physical cruelty during divorce proceedings. Thus, while it would be inaccurate to imply that no legal recourse was available to women who had been raped by their husbands, it is clear that little legal protection was available to married women who had been raped by their husbands.

more, case law specified that the victim had to refuse consent and the perpetrator had to intend to perform the act without the victim's consent in order for the accused to be found guilty of rape. This meant that a man who forced sexual intercourse on a woman without her consent could not be convicted of rape if he had not intended to do it without her consent. This is what is known as the honest-but-mistaken belief in consent defence. Critics of this defence argued that it perpetuated the myth that women mean yes when they say no. So long as a man had the honest-but-mistaken belief that a woman's resistance was not a sign that she was really saying no, that her protests, or failure to offer sufficient physical resistance, etc., were simply signs that she was being coy or playing hard to get, he could not be convicted of rape.

Today, the situation is somewhat different. The criminal code was amended effective January 4, 1983. The offence of rape, as well as the offences of Indecent Assault on a Male and Indecent Assault on a Female, no longer exist.[2] These offences were replaced by a trio of offences: Sexual Assault, Sexual Assault with a Weapon or causing Bodily Harm, and Aggravated Sexual Assault. These new offences are distinguished by the level and type of violence involved. Sexual Assault is the least violent form, while Sexual Assault with a Weapon and Aggravated Sexual Assault are the more violent crimes. Moreover, heterosexual as well as homosexual rape are treated, legally, as equally serious crimes, and married men can no longer claim immunity from prosecution if they rape their wives.

Unfortunately, the 1983 Criminal Code amendments still do not offer definitions acceptable to everyone. First, the 1983 amendments do not provide a specific definition of sexual assault. Second, the law retains the honest-but-mistaken defence.

Even while the law was being debated in the House of Commons, some analysts were critical of its contents. They suggested the lack of a clear definition in the law would result in its uneven application. They were fearful that the police and the courts might interpret similar events as if they were dissimilar (Jackman, 1982; Landau and Lowenberger, 1983; Lowenberger and Landau, 1982). It was not long before researchers found evidence to support this claim (Ellis, 1986; Hinch, 1988a, 1988b, in press). From 1983 to 1985, police investigators and the courts offered wildly differing interpretations of sexual assault.

---

[2] A number of other changes were made at the same time. For a more complete summary of these changes see Hinch (1985).

For example, in one case, a New Brunswick court ruled that un-consented touching of a woman's breasts was a common assault, not a sexual assault. In another case, an Ontario court ruled that unconsented touching of a woman's breast was sexual assault. In 1987, the Supreme Court of Canada offered its interpretation of the legal definition of sexual assault. The Supreme Court stated that sexual assault is:

> ... an assault ... which is committed in circumstances of a sexual nature, such that the sexual integrity of the victim is violated. The test to be applied in determining whether the impugned conduct has the requisite sexual nature is an objective one: 'Viewed in the light of all the circumstances, is the sexual or carnal context of the assault visible to a reasonable observer?' (as cited in Nuttall, 1989: 14).

While this ruling pronounces that an assault must have a clear sexual nature before it can be termed a sexual assault, it still leaves individual police officers, as well as judges and juries, a great amount of discretion in deciding whether or not a given act is a sexual act "in light of the circumstances." This is not an objective test; rather, it is highly subjective. Hinch (1988a; 1988b) shows that police decisions in applying any definition are inconsistent. Similar acts committed in similar circumstances may or may not be treated as sexual assault. The subjective interpretations of individual police officers, judges and juries leads to different interpretations of similar circumstances.

As for the retention of the honest-but-mistaken defence, critics suggested before and after the 1983 amendments that it should have been abolished (Hinch, in press; Landau and Lowenberger, 1983; Ranson, 1982a, 1982b). Retention of this defence in the case of sexual assault perpetuates what Clark and Lewis (1977) termed coercive sexuality. The circumstances which create, for the offender, a mistaken impression that consent has been given are created within the context of a conception of male-female sexual interaction in which men are defined as conquerors and women are defined as objects to be conquered. Maintenance of this conception of male-female interaction contributes to the perpetuation of violence in the form of sexual assault.

However, it can not be ignored that retention of the honest-but-mistaken defence does satisfy some people. For example, the civil libertarians and some criminal lawyers argue that Canadian criminal courts can not be effective if only the intention of the victim were to be considered in criminal cases. They argue that it is a fundamental principle of Canadian criminal law that the offender must have intended to perform the act without the victim's consent in order for it to be judged a sexual assault.

Thus, the dilemma in arriving at a definition of either rape or sexual assault centres on deciding which type of definition is most appropriate. Is it more appropriate to have a definition based on the assumption that any unconsented sexual touching, even if the offender does not intended to do it without consent, is wrong and should be a criminal offence? Or, is it more appropriate to have a definition in which the intent of both the victim and the offender must be taken into account? No matter which definition is used, there will be those who disagree.

We have opted for the former. An event should be legally termed a rape or a sexual assault if it can be shown that it was performed without the consent of the victim. This is the only way to protect people from unwanted sexual acts.

In the section which follows, we will illustrate how different definitions of rape and sexual assault lead to difficulties in determining how much rape and sexual assault occurs, as well has how to theorize about rape and sexual assault.

How Many Canadian People Are Raped and Sexually Assaulted?

The usual method for determining the crime rate is to first count the number of criminal events reported to the police in a given year, subtract the number of events the police determine to be unfounded, divide that number by the estimated population for that year, and, finally, multiply by 100,000. This produces what is known as the rate per 100,000. Using this method, the rates of rape and sexual assault from 1962 to 1988 are shown in Tables 4-1 and 4-2. Note that these tables show that the rape rate almost tripled from 1962 to 1982. Similarly, the sexual assault rate from 1983 to 1988 has almost doubled. This would seem to be a relatively straight forward calculation.

However, several factors must be kept in mind. First, it should be noted that the rates per 100,000 reported in Tables 4-1 and 4-2 are calculated after subtracting the number of the rapes, etc. (as defined in the law) that the police believe to be unfounded. That is, the events the police assess as either false complaints or as noncriminal events are deducted from the offences reported to calculate the offence rate. Thus, the rate per 100,000 reported in these tables is not calculated on the basis of all events reported to the police. It is calculated after deducting the unfounded cases.

TABLE 4-1: Rates of Rape and Indecent Assault, 1962-82

Year	Rape	Indecent Assault on a Female	Indecent Assault on a Male
1962	3.1		
1963	3.5		
1964	4.6		
1965	3.9		
1966	3.2		
1967	3.8		
1968	4.3		
1969	4.9		
1970	5.0		
1971	5.7		
1972	5.9		
1973	7.2		
1974	8.1	23.9[a]	5.2[a]
1975	8.1	22.4	5.1
1976	7.9	22.8	4.8
1977	8.0	2.6	5.7
1978	8.5	24.3	5.2
1979	9.6	25.7	5.8
1980	9.7	27.3	5.4
1981	10.5	27.7	5.2
1982	10.0	29.0	6.0

[a] Data unavailable prior to 1974.

SOURCE: Statistics Canada, Crime and Traffic Statistics, Bulletin: 85-205, 1962-82.

A complication arises via the observation that some of the cases the police dismiss as unfounded may in fact be founded. Research has shown that police judgement that an event is or is not a criminal event often depends as much on police assessments of the victim's reputation as it does on police judgment of the legal merits of the case (Clark and Lewis, 1977; Gunn and Minch, 1988; Hinch, 1988a, 1988b). Clark and Lewis (1977) found that some women are very likely to have their com-

TABLE 4-2: Rates of Sexual Assault, Canada, 1983-88

Year	Sexual Assault	Sexual Assault with a Weapon	Aggravated Sexual Assault
1983	42	3	2
1984	54	3	2
1985	67	3	2
1986	74	4	2
1987	82	4	2
1988	91	4	1

SOURCE: Statistics Canada, Canadian Crime Statitstics Bulletin: 85-205, 1983-88

plaints defined as unfounded by the police. 98 percent of rape cases that involved females they referred to as "women who can't be raped" and as "open territory victims" were dismissed as unfounded. These women were prostitutes, known alcoholics, women who were drinking at the time of the offence, drug users, women on welfare, and unemployed women, as well as women noted in police reports as "idle." Clark and Lewis concluded that almost 74 percent of these women's complaints termed unfounded by the police were potentially founded. If Clark and Lewis's calculations are right, then the rape rate from 1962 to 1982 would have to be increased accordingly. Given that Hinch (1988a; 1988b) also found that these same problems existed as late as 1984, it would also seem necessary to increase the rates reported in Table 4–2.

Furthermore, not all rapes and sexual assaults are reported to the police. The reasons victims do not report their victimization to the police vary. One study, The Canadian Urban Victimization Survey (CUVS) (Solicitor General of Canada, 1985a) found that the three most common reasons victims give for not reporting their sexual victimization are:

1. No benefit would be derived from reporting the incident (52%).

2. The criminal justice system would not be able to help them (45%).

3. Fear of revenge (almost one third).

Another 30 percent gave unspecified reasons for not reporting their victimization.

How many rapes and sexual assaults go unreported to the police? The CUVS found that only 39 percent of all sexual assaults—including rape and other forms of sexual assault—are reported to the police. Thus, 61 percent of sexual assaults go unreported (Solicitor General of Canada, 1985a). However, another Canadian survey estimated that, in any one year, 91 percent of female, and 93 percent of male victims do not report being victimized (Badgley,1984).[3]

There are several reasons for these discrepancies in the estimated rape rate. First, each study used a different definition of rape or sexual assault. Second, each study used a different research methodology.

With regard to the definitions used, the Badgley Committee (Badgley, 1984) used a very broad definition of sexual assault. Threatened as well as actual acts of both exposure and touching were counted as sexual assaults. The CUVS included only acts of actual touching.[4] It is therefore obvious that the results of these surveys are not directly comparable. At best they tell us that there is more unwanted, possibly criminal, sexual touching than is recorded in police files.

Further, we have defined rape and sexual assault in terms that differ from both the legal definitions and the definitions used to complete the surveys. Using our definition, more rapes would be recorded than appear in Table 4-1, or in surveys where rape is defined as vaginal penetration by a penis. There would also be more sexual assault than is indicated in Tables 4-1 and 4-2 because our definition does not exclude instances the police would exclude because it might not satisfy legal requirements. Data reported in Tables 4-1 and 4-2 refer only to cases in which the police believe meet the legal requirement. Our definition, like many surveys, includes any unconsented sexual touching.

With regard to differences in methodology, some victimization surveys use mailed questionnaires, others use telephone interviews, and some use face to face interviews. While each method has its own problems, some common flaws are evident. They all assume that their respondents have accurate memories of the events being reported. This is problematic for several reasons. First, some studies, such as the CUVS, ask respondents to report all incidents perpetrated on them during the previous twelve months. It is possible that some events may be reported that did not occur within this time frame. It is also possible that some

---

[3] Similar studies in the United Sates, estimate that 70 to 93 percent of all rapes go unreported (LeGrande, 1973; Media and Thompson, 1974; Russell, 1984). It would appear, therefore, that, at best, only 70 percent of rapes and only 62 percent of all sexual assaults are reported to the police.

[4] Similarly, Russell (1984), in her study of rape in San Francisco, included only actual acts of unconsented touching.

events occurring within this time frame were forgotten. In other words, faulty memories produce either overestimates or underestimates that can not be verified. Second, they all assume that what they are measuring is a close approximation of what would be considered rape or a sexual assault by the police and the courts. As noted previously, this is a highly questionable assumption. Respondents are more likely to understand the event being reported in their own terms. They may be able to say that they were the victims of unconsented sexual acts, but the legal requirement that the act must also have been intentionally perpetrated without their consent can not be determined. Thus, even though police and court decision making in classifying some events as unfounded is extremely problematic, it is possible that some of the events reported as crimes in these surveys may not have been criminal acts in the legal sense. Of course, those who argue that the legal definition is inappropriate, would argue that the results of these surveys still gives a better indication of how many people are victims of unwanted sexual touching.

Finally, the rate per 100,000 is an estimate of the relative probabilities that someone will be raped or sexually assaulted in a given year. It does not indicate the relative probabilities of someone being raped or sexually assaulted in their lifetime. Consequently, both the Badgley Committee survey (1984) and Russell (1984) sought information concerning the probability of lifetime victimization. Their results appear to be quite similar. The Badgley Committee found that approximately 42 percent of all Canadians, 54 percent of all females and 31 percent of all males, are raped or sexually assaulted at least once in their lifetime. Russell found that 54 percent of her female respondents were raped or sexually assaulted at least once prior to age 18.[5]

However, it should be noted, once again, that these studies used very different definitions of sexual assault. The Badgely Committee's definition includes threats as well as actual acts of unwanted sexual touching of both males and females, while Russell included only incidents of unconsented touching of females. Further, because both studies rely on potentially faulty victim memories; incidents that may have happened in their childhood may have been distorted or forgotten. Furthermore, both rely on common sense conceptions of rape and sexual assault, and

---

[5] It should be noted that sexual victimization as a child has been strongly correlated with entry into prostitution. Both male and female prostitutes have been found to have unusually high rates of sexual abuse as children (James and Meyerling, 1977; Lowman, 1987; Visano, 1987; Weisberg, 1985).

therefore may not satisfy the legal definition. Nonetheless, both studies indicate that women are far more vulnerable to all forms of sexual assault than are men, and that the number of male and female victims is much higher that the rate per 100,000 would indicate.

Patterns of Sexual Assault in Canada

The focus for this section is on describing, in general terms, the victims of rape and sexual assault, the offenders, and the relations between victims and offenders.

The Victim

In constructing a profile of the average victim data relating to sex, age, marital status, socio-economic background, and life style are presented. Each of these variables has an impact on the probability that any one person will or will not be sexually assaulted.

Sex

Whatever the data source, one finding is obvious. More women than men are victimized. Exactly how many more women than men are victimized is not clear. From studies of incidents reported to the police, female victims outnumber male victims by a considerable margin. In Halifax, Hinch (1988a) found that female victims outnumbered male victims almost nine to one in 1982, by almost six to one in 1983, and five to one in 1984. In Toronto, Nuttall (1989) found that female victims constituted 96% of victims known to the police. Survey data, such as those reported in the Badgely Report (1984) and the CUVS (Solicitor General of Canada, 1985a) indicate a similar pattern. The Badgely Committee found that five females are raped or sexually assaulted for every three males, while the CUVS reports a ratio of seven females for every male. Given the general pattern of male and female sex roles, this should not be surprising.

Age

While it is clear that victims may range from infants to the elderly, the average victim, whether male or female, tends to be under 30. These results are consistently reported in both victimization surveys and studies based on police records (Amir, 1971; Clark and Lewis, 1977; Gun and Minch, 1988; Hinch, 1988a, 1988b; McCahill, 1979; Nuttall, 1989; Media and Thompson, 1974; Hindelang and Davis, 1977; Russell, 1984; Solicitor General of Canada, 1985a; Badgley, 1984). Some studies even show that the majority of the victims reported to the police are 17 or under (Gunn and Minch, 1988; Hinch 1988b). In addition, some surveys have discovered that more than half of all the respondents claim that the first time they were sexually assaulted they were 16 or under, and that up to 80 percent were under 21 (Badgley, 1984; Russell, 1984). Victims over 30 account for between 11 percent (Gunn and Minch, 1988) and 30 percent (Amir, 1971; Clark and Lewis, 1977) of known victims. Thus, despite the differences in definition and research methodologies, there seems to be agreement that the average victim is under 30, and that the most frequent victims are between the ages of 16 and 24.[6]

Marital Status

Given the age range of victims, it is not surprising that more single than married people are victimized. Police studies and victimization surveys consistently show that between 70 and 91 percent of all sexual assault victims, including those of rape, are single or divorced (Amir, 1971; Clark and Lewis, 1977; Gunn and Minch, 1988; Hindelang and Davis, 1977; McCahill et al., 1979; Media and Thompson, 1974; Nuttall, 1989). In Gunn and Minch's study, only 9 percent were married or living as married, while 12 percent were divorced or widowed. Nuttall found that almost 20 percent were married or living with male companions.

These studies, however, account for only those victims found in police records and may, as a result, underestimate the number of married women who are raped by their husbands. Russell (1982, 1984) shows that many married women do not report husbands who rape them. Indeed, studies of wife abuse in general have found that married women frequently do not report their abusive husbands (see Chapter 2). Even though there is some risk for women who do not report the abusive behaviour of their husbands, there is also some risk in reporting that behaviour. They risk the loss of economic security, including the loss of the family home, as well as further abuse once their husbands are released from police custody.

Exactly how many married women are sexually assaulted by their husbands is difficult to determine (see the section on The Victim/Offender Relation). Nonetheless, it would appear that the percentage of

---

[6] An interesting exception to this general pattern is found in the Nuttall (1989) study of incidents reported in 1985 to the Toronto police. Nuttall found that the average of the victims known to Toronto police was 27. However, the Nuttall study excluded all incidents in which the victim was under 16; therefore, her results are not comparable to the other studies, which included victims under 16.

married women who are raped is higher than some victim surveys and police data indicate.

Socio-Economic Background

The data on the socio-economic background of victims shows a consistent pattern. Most victims come from lower socio-economic backgrounds (Clark and Lewis, 1977; Ageton, 1983; CUVS, 1983; Badgley, 1984). These studies reveal that even though rape and sexual assault occur at all socio-economic levels, about 60 percent or more of known victims, especially in police records, are from lower socio-economic groups. For example, Clark and Lewis (1977) found that at least 57 percent of the victims in their study were on welfare, prostitutes, unemployed, clerical or factory workers, domestic servants, waitresses, or sales clerks. Only 7 percent of the victim's in their study were classified as "professionals." However, they may have underestimated the percentage of victims in their study who were from lower socio-economic groups. They note that approximately 18 percent were students, 15 percent were housewives, and 3 percent were retired. Some of these people may be from lower socio-economic groups.

It is interesting to note as well that the Badgely Committee survey found that 43 percent of child sexual assaults reported to the Toronto police involved victims who were living in public housing (Badgley, 1984).[7] This may in part be the result of what some researchers have referred to as the overpolicing of these communities. Because these communities are said to be high crime areas, it is possible that the police, and others including social workers coming in contact with welfare recipients, may pay closer attention to all forms of criminal activity in these areas than they would in other neighbourhoods.

Life Style

Some types of sexual assault seem to be related to factors associated with life style. For example, the CUVS found that "The reported incidence of sexual assault was highest for those who attended the greatest number of evening activities outside the home" (1985a: 3). It seems that most victims are attacked in public places. However, other studies indicate that this may be true only of those sexual assaults that do not involve penetration. Actual rapes are more likely to occur indoors. Police records and victimization surveys report that somewhere between

---

[7]   Similar studies in the U.S. also indicate that residents of public housing seem to be overrepresented among victims known to the police (McCahill, et al., 1979: 8).

55 and 87 percent of all rapes occur indoors in the home of the victim, the home of an acquaintance, or the offender's home (Amir, 1971; Clark and Lewis, 1977; Hindelang and Davis, 1977; McCahill and Davis, 1977; McCaldon, 1967; Media and Thompson, 1974). The wide range in percentage of attacks occurring indoors versus outdoors is attributed to differences in data sources and definitions used.

The Offender

Providing a description of the average offender is more difficult than offering a description of the average victim. Less is known about the offender than is known about the victim. While it is possible to ask people if they have been victimized, it is a far more difficult task to ask them to report how many people they have raped or sexually assaulted. Moreover, a significant number of victims can not identify their offenders. Therefore, given that more than half, perhaps as many as 80 percent of all offenders are unknown, it is difficult to offer as complete a description of the offender as it is of the victim. Thus, the data that follows must be interpreted with great care.

Sex

One certainty about offenders is that they are overwhelmingly male—even in instances where males are the victims. Police files rarely record a female offender.[8] Russell (1984) and Finkelhor (1984) indicate that in those child sexual abuse cases where a female perpetrator is reported to the police she is usually an accomplice to a male offender. Both the Badgley Report (1984) and Finkelhor (1984) indicate that less than 1.5 percent of known offenders are female.

Age

Offenders identified in police records are usually slightly older than their victims. Most studies of police files indicate that the majority of rapists are under 30 (Amir, 1971; MacDonald, 1971; Chappell and Singer, 1977). Only Clark and Lewis (1977) found that a significant number of rapists, slightly more than 40 percent, were over 30.

---

[8] One of these rare occurrences was reported to police in Guelph, Ontario in November, 1989. A 27 year old man claimed that he had been walking home when three women stopped their car and offered him a ride. He accepted, but once in the car, the driver pointed a gun at him and all three sexually assaulted him. Other than the title of the story, the details reported in the news media did not specify the type of sexual assault committed ("City man claims rape at gunpoint" (*The Daily Mercury*, November 29, 1990: 1).

Different age groups commit different acts. Nuttall (1989) found that offenders aged 12 to 18 are the least likely to commit acts of penetration, but the most likely to be involved in other acts of touching. Offenders 20 to 29 are more likely to commit acts of penetration, and the least likely to be involved in other acts of touching.

Marital Status

The best available data on the marital status of offenders comes from studies using police records, which are notorious for not including all offenders. Indeed, in most incidents reported to the police, the offender is not identified. Bearing these important qualifications in mind, the majority of rapists known to the police are single. For example, Nuttall (1989) reports that 58 percent of men arrested for sexual assault, including rape, by Toronto police in 1985 were single, while Amir (1971) found that almost two thirds were single.[9]

Socio-Economic Background

Some researchers have argued that "almost without exception the rapists in our study came from lower socio-economic groups" (Clark and Lewis, 1977: 98). However, their data base is extremely limited. Missing from their data base are all those offenders who were not reported to the police, as well as all those offenders who were not identified by either the victim or the police. Therefore, since the majority of offenders can not be identified, it is difficult to offer a definitive statement about the socio-economic background of offenders. Nonetheless, we can discuss what is known about offenders known to the police. There are some similarities in the backgrounds of known rapists and their victims. Known rapists come from the same class backgrounds as their victims (Schwendinger and Schwendinger, 1983; Russell, 1984).

If this is true, several explanations are possible. First, people from similar socio-economic backgrounds are more likely to come in contact with each other. Therefore, since they live in the same neighbourhoods, go to the same recreational areas, attend parties, etc., with others from the same background, and have mutual friends and acquaintances, it

---

[9]   In one of the few victim surveys attempting to describe the marital status of the average offender, Media and Thompson (1974) found that the victim's believed that 38 percent of the offenders were single, 11 percent were believed to be separated, and 18 percent were believed to be married. But these findings can not be trusted. Not only do they rely on the victim's impression of the offender's marital status, but one third of the victim's could not determine the marital status of the offender.

would seem consistent that rapist and victim would come from the same socio-economic background. Caution, however, must be exercised before making any definitive statement. Too little is known about the majority who go undetected and remain unknown.

The Victim-Offender Relation

Information concerning the victim/offender relation comes, once again, from studies of police records and victimization surveys. As expected, the data are not consistent. If we rely solely on police records, most sexual assaults are committed by strangers. But survey research indicates that most sexual assaults are committed by persons known to the victim. Therefore, caution is needed in describing the typical victim-offender relation.

U.S. studies of police records indicate that somewhere between 42 (Amir, 1971) and 72 percent (Duncan and Singer, 1977) of rapists reported to the police are strangers to the victim. The discrepancies between these studies and the Canadian studies may be accounted for via examination of the definitions used. In the Clark and Lewis study, "stranger" refers to offenders whom the victim met for the first time on the day of the rape. Amir referred to these men as "acquaintances," a term Clark and Lewis limit to men who were only casually known to the victim as friends of other friends, etc. Thus, some of those offenders classified by Clark and Lewis as "strangers," Amir classified as "acquaintances." The difference is obvious. If the Amir definition is used, a lower percentage of stranger rapes is determined, but if the Clark and Lewis definition is used, a higher percentage of stranger rapes is determined.

Canadian research found that 64 percent of rapes reported to the police are committed by strangers (Clark and Lewis, 1977), and that approximately 48 percent of all sexual assaults reported to the police are committed by strangers (Nuttall, 1989). In Nuttall's study, 23 percent were committed by acquaintances, 2 percent by friends, 13 percent by ex-husbands or boyfriends, 2 percent by family members, 6 percent by bosses, etc., and 8 percent by clients of prostitutes: Note that, unless husbands are included among friends and/or family members, none of the offenders arrested were husbands of the victim.

But this only accounts for those incidents reported to the police, and it is well known that victims of sexual assault are less likely to report incidents in which the offender is known to them (Solicitor General of Canada, 1985a; Russell, 1984; Badgley, 1984; Gunn and Minch, 1988). For example, Gunn and Minch (1988) found that while 75 percent of sexual assaults committed by strangers are reported to the police, only

25 percent of sexual assaults committed by family members are reported to the police. These findings show that the closer the relation between the victim and the offender, the less likely it is that the incident will be reported to the police. Similar findings were also obtained by the CUVS. Interestingly, while persons known to the victim are less likely to be reported to the police, some research shows that persons known to the victim are more likely to be arrested. Nuttall (1989) found that seven out of every ten offenders known to the victim were arrested, while only three out of every ten strangers were arrested. Persons known to the victim are more likely to be arrested because it is easier for police to identify, locate and apprehend them.

The full extent of the over-representation of strangers in police files is more visible in Russell's (1984) study. Fifty-one percent of rapes are committed by dates, boyfriends, lovers or ex-lovers and husbands, 4 percent are committed by relatives, 13 percent by either family friends or friends of the victim, and 7 percent by persons in authority (employers, teachers, etc.). Strangers account for only 16 percent of all rapists. While other studies have not uncovered as much rape by persons in authority, their data on the high percentage of unreported family and close friends, and the low percentage of stranger rapes are consistent with Russell's findings (Lott, et al., 1982).

It is also important to note that children seem to be particularly vulnerable to being sexually assaulted by persons known to them. Police studies are more likely to reveal a larger number of strangers sexually assaulting children, but survey data indicates a higher percentage of such attacks come from persons in positions of control or authority, such as teachers, guardians, babysitters, relatives, etc. (Badgley, 1984).

To summarize the relation between the victim and the offender, while discrepancies exist in the literature, these discrepancies may be accounted for via reference to the differences in data sources. Studies of police files indicate a higher percentage of sexual assaults by strangers because victims feel less social pressure to conceal these attacks than when the attacker is someone they know. Overall, the closer the victim-offender relation is, the less likely the attack will be reported to the police. Moreover, the majority of all sexual assaults are committed by persons known to the victim; even if they are not necessarily well-known. The offenders are dates, boyfriends, lovers, ex-lovers, husbands, ex-husbands, relatives, friends, family friends, babysitters, teachers, and employers.

Theories of Sexual Assault

The following section focuses on various explanations of sexual assault. The theories examined here include control theory, interactionist theory, feminist theory and Marxian theory. The intention in reviewing these theories goes beyond the mere act of critique. Our purpose is to argue that a feminist informed Marxist theory offers a superior explanation of sexual assault.

Control Theories

Control theorists assume that the deviant is inappropriately socialized. He or she has not been exposed to socially accepted standards of behaviour. Consequently, the deviant sets his/her own behaviour standards, which may actually be reinforced by others who behave in a similar pattern. When applied as an explanation of sexual assault, it is argued that the offender either has not been taught to relate to others, especially women, in a non-violent, non-aggressive manner, or has learned that his aggressive, violent behaviour may actually get him what he wants (Cormier and Simons, 1969; Marcus, 1969; Marshall 1973; Marshall and McKnight 1975; Groth, 1979). Acting on what control theorists regard as a natural tendency towards self gratification, placing personal interests above the interests of others, the offender seeks to achieve personal gratification at the expense of the victim.

Control theorists, however, are careful to point out that the gratification sought by the rapist is not necessarily sexual gratification. The rapist seems to be more concerned with the ability to control and dominate the victim than he is with achieving sexual satisfaction (Gebhard, et al., 1965; Rada, 1978; Groth, 1979). Many attempted rapes fail because the attacker has difficulty obtaining an erection, or reaching orgasm. Their objective is to achieve self-enhancement through the degradation and humiliation of the victim. Even in gang rape situations, the primary satisfaction is the camaraderie experienced among the rapists (Groth, 1979). Whether on his own, or with other gang rapists, the rapist is seeking to control the victim, and convince himself and his male peers of his superiority.

That is not to suggest that control theorists believe that some rapists do not experience sexual gratification through rape. Gebhard et al. (1965), and Rada (1978) argue that many rapists are sexually motivated. They rape when their efforts at persuasion fail. However, even some of these rapists may express hostile attitudes towards women. They divide women into two groups: those who deserve respect, and those who do not. Rape is a mechanism for controlling "bad" women.

Rapists learn to be a rapists, according to control theorists, through association with other males in what are sometimes called masculinity contests. The object of these contests is the sexual domination of women. While teenage males are particularly vulnerable to peer pressure, adult men also feel the pressure, even after marriage, to experience a variety of sexual partners, and activities.

To summarize, control theorists argue that the probability that a man will become a rapists depends upon some combination of the following:

1. The extent to which males have been taught to be domineering and aggressive in their interactions with females.

2. The extent to which group pressure influences males to keep pace with the real or imagined sexual exploits of their peers.

3. The extent to which males have been successfully taught the necessary skills to participate in mutually consenting interactions with females.

Critique

There are two major problems with this perspective. First, the rapists who are used to provide empirical support for it are almost always those who have been caught and processed by the criminal justice system, or have been confined to mental institutions. Consequently, given that only a small proportion of the total number of rapists come in contact with the criminal justice system, they are not representative of all rapists. Until more is known about the rapists who do not come in contact with the criminal justice system and other social control agencies, it is impossible to determine the extent to which these men and their orientations toward women are representative of either all rapists or of all men.

From our viewpoint the most important shortcoming of this perspective is its explanation of the origins of the anti-woman values rapists are said to possess. The perspective contends that the individual naturally engages in self-satisfying, anti-social behaviour until taught to behave otherwise. Even to the extent that this perspective acknowledges that some forms of anti-social behaviour are learned from others who act in anti-social ways, it still relies on the notion that the anti-social behaviour of others simply reinforces the individual's predisposition to such behaviour.

We reject the notion that human behaviour is shaped by a natural predisposition towards deviance. Instead, we argue that human behaviour is shaped by the material circumstances in which people live out their lives. In this context, the rapist's behaviour is determined by the existence of a political-economic system in which individualism, competitiveness and domination are the guiding principles. North Americans, for example, live in a political economic system that is both patriarchal and capitalist. As such, our institutions, the family, the economy, etc., are based on the notion of individual gain through the domination of others. Rapists' attempts to exert control and dominate women are not simply reflections of natural tendencies toward self-satisfaction, but a direct result of the transmission of values derived from both patriarchal and capitalist value structures.

Interactionist Theory

The starting point for understanding the interactionist approach to the analysis of sexual assault is the recognition that people interact on the basis of shared meanings. As long as the meanings of social actions and interactions are shared, relationships are stable and free of conflict. It is when meanings are not shared, or when actions are interpreted differently by the participants that problems arise.

For example, Klemmack and Klemmack (1976) argue that conventional sex-role modelling is a significant factor leading to rape. At times, neither men nor women fully appreciate their own or others actions and reactions. According to Klemmack and Klemmack, the concept of femininity contains two contradictory elements. On the one hand, it emphasizes passivity, receptiveness, and innocence, especially in relation to sexual encounters. On the other hand, it may include notions of being seductive, coy and flirtatious. More importantly, women are supposed to use these contradictory traits to solicit attention and favours from men. In contrast, masculinity emphasizes male conquest of women. Men are taught to expect sexual rewards for the attention and material favours they bestow on women. Therefore, especially when men and women interact in dating relations, problems related to interpreting the actions of others, whether verbal or non-verbal, increase the potential for misunderstood intentions and rape.

Because situations may be interpreted differently by men and women, some interactionists claim that some rapes are victim- precipitated. The researcher most noted for development of this concept is Amir (1971), but other researchers have also contributed to its development (Ageton, 1983; Curtis, 1973; Gaudet, 1984; Klemmack and Klemmack, 1976). Collectively, these theorists argue that women put themselves at risk by doing things, intentionally or unintentionally, which may be interpreted as a "come on" by the rapist, or as deliberate risk taking by others. According to Amir (1971), 19 percent of all rapes are victim precipitated. Other researchers estimate that only four percent are victim-precipitated (Curtis, 1973).

Most of the research on this concept concentrates on clarifying the types of situations that may be called victim precipitated. In general terms, Amir argued that victim- precipitation occurs in situations "marred by sexuality."

Victim-precipitated rapes result from the following situations.

1. The victim and the offender consume alcohol together prior to the rape—35 percent of victim-precipitated rapes are of this type according to Amir (1971: 271).

2. The victim consumes alcohol, either alone or with others, prior to being raped—18 percent of victim precipitated rapes are of this type says Amir (1971: 271).

3. Females were hitchhiking. While a percentage is not given, Nelson and Amir (1977: 288) contend that the incidence of rape would be reduced " ... if there were no hitchhiking females."

4. Instances where the victim voluntarily goes to a man's home, or invites a man to her home.

5. The rapist believes, or is lead to believe, that the victim has a reputation for promiscuity, or for engaging in other forms of deviant behaviour. Ageton (1983), for example, found that adolescent females were more likely than non-delinquent females to be sexually assaulted.

Thus, whether or not women intend their actions in these situations to be interpreted as sexual "come ons," their actions may be interpreted as such by men.

In summary, interactionists analyze rape as a product of situations in which one or both parties misunderstood the situation. Both have misinterpreted the actions of the other, and may also have misunderstood how the other would react to them. These misunderstandings result from such factors as the definitions of femininity and masculinity where femininity is defined in terms of passivity and receptiveness and masculinity is defined in terms of domination and aggression. Rape occurs when men interpret women's actions as implied consent.

Critique

The most significant shortcoming of this theory is its failure to account for less serious forms of sexual assault. While it is true that some rapes result from misunderstood communication, it is equally true that many rapes and other sexual assaults occur in situations where the attacker knows from the beginning that he will rape or sexually assault the victim. This is especially true in cases of minor sexual assaults where the offender grabs a woman's breast, or touches her genitals then runs away. In almost one half of all rapes reported to the police, the rapist made his intentions known at the initial contact with his victim. Therefore, these situations can not be interpreted as misunderstood communications, or as situations with ambiguous meanings.

As for the notion of victim-precipitation, it has been severely criticized, even by some interactionists (Sanders, 1980) for implying that the victim is responsible for the actions of the offender. It is important to note that Amir borrowed the concept of victim-precipitation from Wolfgang's (1958) explanation for certain types of murder. Wolfgang used it to explain those murders in which the victim intended to provoke a specific response from the offender by behaving in ways the victim knew would elicit that response. But as Amir uses it, it also refers to actions which the victim did not intend to provoke. This extension of the concept is unwarranted. It implies that the victim is responsible for the actions of the offender.

Feminist Theory

The feminist theory of rape begins with the acknowledgment that patriarchy is the root cause of rape. Patriarchy gives rise to a system of rigid gender-role models in which men are assigned active, aggressive roles, while women are assigned passive, receptive roles. The values inherent in these gender roles are transmitted and reinforced through the institutions of patriarchy, especially the family and the law. The family encourages women to place their needs in subordination to the needs of their families, and encourages men to assume that their economic dominance also bestows sexual dominance. The law, including law enforcement practices, makes it clear that women are the sexual property of men both in and out of marriage. Within marriage, the law makes it difficult for women to resist the sexual demands of their husbands. Outside of marriage, when women attempt to live lives independently of men, law enforcement practices encourage men to sexually assault these unprotected women.

One of the early feminist theorists, Brownmiller (1975), argued that women's subjugation began in the first human societies when they surrendered the right to say no to one man in exchange for his protection against attack from all other men. This "protective conjugal relationship"

(1975: 17), which is now known as the monogamous marriage, became and remains a mechanism by which women become the property, especially the sexual property, of men. In early patriarchal societies, a raped woman, because she had lost her virginity, became less valuable to her father. He could no longer receive the same bride price for her. Thus, to reinforce his claim to ownership of his daughter's sexuality, including her reproductive capacity, a father could collect a fine from the rapist as compensation for damage to the father's property.

This early arrangement may be said to survive in contemporary legal definitions of rape. For example, in many states of the United States, and in Canada until 1983, men could not be prosecuted for raping their wives. These criminal statutes specifically defined rape as unconsented intercourse with female persons other than the rapist's wife. Furthermore, feminists, such as Clark and Lewis (1977), and Gunn and Minch (1988), found that women who have independent (e.g., not under the protection of men) lifestyles, or who behave in ways which are believed to be disreputable for women (prostitutes and alcoholics, for example), are significantly less likely than other women to be believed when they claim to have been raped. These researchers' studies of police enforcement practices and court decisions indicate that unprotected women, or disreputable women, are either unlikely to see their case taken to trial, or unlikely to see a guilty verdict if it does go to trial. The point is that rape and the threat of rape are used as control mechanisms. They serve as a reminder to both reputable and disreputable women that they are vulnerable to sexual assault whether they are married or unmarried, reputable or disreputable. Respectable, married women may receive better protection than other women from men other than their husbands, but husbands too may rape or sexually assault them.

Another way in which contemporary society encourages rape is found in the way men and women are encouraged to behave prior to and during sexual encounters. Similar to the interactionists, feminists, like Clark and Lewis (1977), argue that a pattern of coercive sexuality persists encouraging sexual assault by turning sexual relations into a battleground. On the one hand, women, who are portrayed as possessing a passive sexuality, and as sexual objects in need of male protection and domination, are expected to offer at least initial resistance to men's sexual advances. But women are also expected to surrender their sexuality in exchange for economic security. On the other hand, men, portrayed as more sexually aggressive and active, are expected to respond to women's verbal rejections, and perhaps even physical resistance, by pressing the issue further. "No" becomes "not yet," and eventually "yes."

Men offer material rewards only if persuasion does not work. In this context, women who step outside the ascribed boundaries of their gender-role, who attempt to live without the protection of family, or husband, and who live life styles that emphasize their independence from male control, place themselves at risk.

It is this accepted pattern of coercive sexuality that lead Griffin (1971) to declare rape the "all American crime." This means that the typical rapist is no different from the average man. He may even be seen as more of a man than the average man. For example, Clark and Lewis (1977), summarizing research on known rapists, say that this research indicates that rapists show no greater tendency towards mental illness than do other men. The principle difference between rapists and other men would appear to be that they are more aggressive and more violent, and have a greater tendency towards accepting the need to dominate women. Known rapists believe themselves to be committing acts of seduction and not acts of violence. This point is crucial in understanding the rapist as the average man. As Smart (1976) explains, the concept of the rapist as the average man depends upon acceptance of certain cultural expectations of men and male sexuality. Male sexuality and aggression appear inextricably linked. To say that the average man and the average rapist are similar is to say that both engage in aggressive behaviour in pursuit of sexual activity. They differ only to the extent that rapists tend to be more violent in this pursuit.

The perpetuation of various rape mythologies also encourages rape. The notion that women like to be raped, and the corresponding linkage of sexuality and violence serve as social encouragements allowing men to ignore women's protests and women to believe that there is no freedom from the threat of rape. The threat of rape and the use of force during rape and other forms of sexual assault discredits the notion that these acts are sex crimes. They are crimes of violence. The notion that women's rape fantasies indicate that women secretly wish to be raped ignores that in any fantasy the person creating it has total control over the situation, while the person being attacked in real life situations has no control. Female sexual fantasies rarely involve violence. The use of violence is frightening to women. It not only involves loss of sexual freedom, it potentially means the loss of one's life. Violence also humiliates victims.

Critique

While there is no doubt that feminist theorizing has contributed greatly to contemporary understandings of sexual assault, there are certain problems with the feminist theory of sexual assault. For example, LaFree (1989) challenges the feminist suggestion that women who engage in inappropriate gender role behaviour will usually meet with little success in having their complaints concluded with a conviction in jury trials. While LaFree agrees that the victim's behaviour is frequently an inappropriate method used by juries to assess guilt (i.e, to blame the victim), his analysis also indicates that this is not always the case. In instances where the major legal issues in the case centre on identification or the defendant's diminished responsibility (e.g., those instances where the victim invites the offender to her home), the data indicates that very few questions are asked about the victim's reputation or sexual history, and that juries convict on the basis of the legal issues.

A second criticism addresses the argument that sexual assault laws seem to benefit only men. While there is no question that these laws, and law enforcement practices, function in ways that are detrimental to women, it is inaccurate to say or to imply that women receive no benefit. Even though the law may be said, historically, to define women as the sexual property of men, contemporary law nonetheless says that women are not to be sexually assaulted. Men are arrested, prosecuted and convicted for sexual assault. While legal intervention may not occur as often as some feminists might like, it does happen. The fact that the law says that sexual assault is a criminal offence, and that some men are arrested, prosecuted and convicted, are indications that women receive some benefit, even if that benefit needs to be improved.

A third criticism, centres on the feminist analysis of the law enforcement process. While feminists have frequently said that low arrest and conviction rates are the product of patriarchy, the law is differentially enforced against men from lower socio-economic groups. That is, the law is created not only to protect patriarchal interests, but also class interests. By concentrating on arresting, prosecuting and convicting men from lower socio-economic groups, the law enforcement process helps perpetuate the myth that it is lower class men who are the threat to personal security. From our vantage point, it is necessary to analyze both the patriarchal and class nature of sexual assault law and law enforcement practices.

Marxist Theory

Like feminists, Marxists argue that it is impossible to understand sexual assault and sexual assault legislation without understanding socio-economic structures and the place of women within those structures. Unlike feminists, Marxists argue that the temptation to explain rape and sexual assault as simply a product of patriarchal relations must be resisted. Rape and sexual assault are products of patriarchal and capitalist relations. Within this context the legal definition and control of sexual violence must also be understood as serving both patriarchal and capitalist interests.[10]

Gender differentiation is universal and is at least as important as class differences (Maroney and Luxton, 1987). Patriarchy gives rise to a system of rigid gender role models, and the values inherent in them are transmitted and reinforced through the family and the state. Failure to understand the role women play in reproduction leads to failure in understanding why rape occurs.

Gender differences also exist across classes. Women's public labour market activities are similar to their roles within the family. Women work primarily in occupations and careers which see them in subordinate or nurturant positions. Three out of four women work either in clerical/sales, or service positions such as teaching and nursing (Parliament, 1990). They are under-represented in positions of power and influence. In effect, women in all class positions have a great deal in common: their subordinate position relative to the men in their class. But their class position also limits their potential to have the kinds of careers, etc., open to men in their class. As members of the working classes, they are less likely to finish high school and less likely to go to university. In fact, they are more likely to work on assembly lines in factories, to have careers as waitresses in "greasy spoon" restaurants, and to work as career sales clerks in places like cheap department stores. Like men in their class, they have less control over their life chances than do women in higher class positions. As Smith (1985) says, the structure of the family in each class determines the type of work women do within the class.

The implication of these observations for the analysis of rape and sexual assault should be clear. Because women occupy lesser positions in both the family and the economy, they lack the social, ideological, political, and economic power that men enjoy. As Schwendinger and Schwendinger (1983), and Messerschmidt (1986) have argued, the advantages men derive from being in these powerful positions allows them to define and control patterns of interaction between the sexes. Men's needs are given first priority, and women's sexuality is subordi-

---

[10] In constructing our argument, we have relied upon such diverse sources as Schwendinger and Schwendinger (1983), Hartsock (1983), Messerschmidt (1986), Armstrong and Armstrong (1983), and, Maroney and Luxton (1987), among others.

nated to men's. Prostitution is overwhelmingly a female occupation because women's sexuality within a capitalist economy becomes a saleable service. Rape and sexual assault offenders are overwhelmingly male because they have the social, ideological, political, and economic power to define their pattern of aggressive sexuality as the universal pattern. Without their power-bases within the family and the economy, men would not have the ability to define and control women's sexuality in terms that subordinate it to men's sexuality.

That is not to say that women are without power. Nor is it to suggest that some women are not more powerful than some men. Women have some power within patriarchal capitalist societies, and this power is not confined to women's traditional power base within the family unit. As Hinch (1988b; in press) and others (Bill C–127 Working Group, 1982) have argued, the amendments to the Criminal Code of Canada abolishing the charge of rape and introducing the trio of sexual assault charges, were introduced in response to a concerted feminist lobby. While it is true, as Snider (1985) and Hinch (in press) point out, that other interests are also represented in the amendments, it is nonetheless true that women were able to effect changes in the law that gave at least symbolic recognition that heterosexual rape and sexual assault constitutes violence against women, and not violence against men's property. Women may be less powerful, but they are not without power.

In this context, a brief word is needed about the way Marxists assess the policing of rape and sexual assault. It is clear from the analysis provided by Clark and Lewis (1977), and supported by Hinch (1988a, 1988b), that certain women lack credibility when they report their victimization to the police. These women include prostitutes, women on welfare, alcoholics, women who were drinking at the time of the offence, unemployed women and women the police record as "idle." As interpreted by Clark and Lewis, the lack of credibility these women have within police departments is simply a product of their non-conformity to stereotypical female role models within a patriarchal society. It is possible, however, to offer a companion, or complementary interpretation.

These women lacked credibility not just because their behaviour was inconsistent with patriarchal values, but also because they lacked the social status and power of women in higher classes. Note that Clark and Lewis found that women who were working, and "professional" women, are more likely than other women to be believed by the police. This clearly introduces a class variable to the equation. Women from higher socio-economic groups have more credibility than women from lower socio-economic groups simply because they are members of a higher class. As members of this higher class, their behaviour patterns, beliefs, etc., are more consistent with the values and beliefs enshrined in the law. They enjoy the credibility that comes from being a member of that class.

Finally, consistent with the overall pattern of enforcing criminal law in a manner detrimental to working class people (see Taylor, 1981; Chambliss and Seidman, 1982), the rape and sexual assault laws are also enforced in this manner. Snider (1985), and many non-Marxist researchers (recall the previous discussion on known offenders), point out that working class men are overrepresented in arrest and conviction rates. Some research has even shown that judges are more tolerant of offenders who approximate the judges in terms of economic status (Barrett and Marshall, 1990).

Thus, even though it is well established that men in all classes rape and sexually assault women, law enforcement practices continue to concentrate on offences committed by the working class. In far too many cases, offences committed by employers are processed as non-criminal events. For example, forced sex, and threats of forced sex on the job are treated as sexual harassment, rather than rape or sexual assault (see Chapter 5). This allows those who abuse their positions of power to escape criminal prosecution. It may be true that they are prosecuted under civil law, or via sexual harassment/civil rights law, but violation of these laws is not perceived to convey the same degree of responsibility, or danger to society, as violation of criminal law.

Policy Issues

There is a long list of initiatives needed to reduce the rate of sexual violence in Canada. At the top of the list is the need to abolish both patriarchy and capitalism. However, the kind of revolution needed to do that seems a distant dream. Other, less perfect, middle range solutions, which offer immediate, or at least foreseeable changes, appear more practical. There is much that can be done now to reduce the rate of victimization, as well as alter the way in which Canadian society deals with victims and offenders. In addition to the middle range solutions noted in Chapters 2 and 3, there are changes needed in the law and the manner in which the police and the courts deal with rape and sexual assault.

The Middle Range Solutions

Because middle range solutions are discussed in some detail in Chapters 2 and 3, only brief comment will be made here. It is self-evident that there is a great deal that men can do to reduce the rate of sexual violence. Just as women have taken the initiative to create awareness among women that they need not be victimized, men can initiate similar efforts to create the awareness among men that they need not be victimizers.

The task will not be easy. Aggressive behaviour is an integral part of male behaviour in both patriarchal and capitalist value structures. Nonetheless, the effort must be made. The kinds of self-help discussion groups often used in the so-called treatment of abusive husbands needs to be expanded to include not just convicted rapists but all men. This does not imply that all men are abusive or rapists. Rather, it implies that men must take responsibility for changing their own patterns. So long as men as a group maintain and perpetuate aggression as a preferred method of obtaining individual or collective goals, rape and sexual assault will remain a feature of social life.

The Legal Issues

The Criminal Code amendments introduced in 1983 were heralded by their advocates as a step forward for women. Critics of the new law, however, were quick to point out shortcomings. They noted problems with the definition of sexual assault, the retention of the honest-but-mistaken believe in consent defence, and the methods of police investigation. These problems are reviewed here with the objective of making suggestions for change.

The Legal Definitions

The major problem with the definition of sexual assault as it is currently defined in the criminal code is the manner in which it is assumed to be gender-neutral. The objective of gender-neutral terminology is defensible, but the solution offered in the law is unacceptable. At present, the law treats some rapes as equivalent to some forms of sexual assault in which the offender grabs a woman's breast, or a victim's (male or female) genitals then runs away. Even the possibility that these minor incidents of sexual assault can be processed via summary procedure rather than indictment, does not solve the problem. Some incidents of rape are also processed via summary conviction procedures.

It is more appropriate to define two separate offences: one for incidents in which penetration is involved, and one for offences not involving penetration. The term rape should be reintroduced and redefined to include any incident involving penetration of the vagina, the anus (male or female), or the mouth (male or female) by any object (a finger, a hand, a penis, a stick, a bottle, etc.) for the purpose of committing a sexual act. This would maintain gender-neutrality, as well as distinguish rape from the grab and run offences.

The amount of violence used in the commission of this redefined rape offence could be recognized in a similar fashion to the way the level of violence is recognized in the current sexual assault law. There could be three separate offences. First, rape would constitute the least violent offence. Second, rape with a weapon or causing bodily harm or threats to a third party would constitute a more serious offence signifying an escalation in the level of violence. Third, aggravated rape would constitute the offence with the most violence. The current sexual assault categories could then be used to designate all other types of sexual assault according to the levels of violence used in their commission.

Defining the offences in this way would not necessarily constitute a return to making the sexual nature of the offence more prominent. To begin with, the sexual nature of the offence remains prominent even in the current legal definition. It is, after all, the sexual nature of the offences that separate them from the common assault offences of assault, assault with a weapon or causing bodily harm, and aggravated assault. To argue that the current law gives less prominence to the sexual nature of the offence because it has been placed in the offences against the person, rather than the sexual offences section of the Criminal Code, or because it no longer requires proof of penetration, is legalistic gamesmanship. It does not matter in which section of the code the offence is placed. What matters is that the amount of violence used to commit the offence be recognized, and that the act of violent penetration be symbolically recognized as always being a more serious offence than grab and run offences, or some other first level sexual assaults in which there is no penetration.

Finally, retention of a separate rape offence would also symbolically recognize that rape still exists, and that it can not be masked by giving it a new name. As Cohen and Backhouse (1980: 6) argue:

> We only want rape to disappear if the crime itself goes away. In a completely nonsexist society, rape would be unthinkable. But since our culture generates rape, a peculiar overlap of violence and sex, we don't want to see that reality swept under the rug. To eliminate the word would not eliminate rape itself.

Rape remains an integral part of everyday language. To assume that it will have lost its meaning just because the law no longer recognizes it as an offence label, assumes a more powerful role for law than can be justifiably assumed. Rather than abandon use of rape entirely, it makes more sense to recognize that it is perceived to be a serious offence, by victims, offenders and the general public, and to expand the definition in the manner suggested.

The Honest-But-Mistaken Defence

There are two arguments in favour of retention of the honest-but-mistaken-belief in consent defence. First, its retention allows the accused the right of a full defence. Second, since it is an essential element of the justice system that the accused must have intended to commit the offence, it must follow that it is necessary to prove that the offender intended to commit rape or sexual assault without the victim's consent. Neither of these arguments can be supported. Both amount to legalized victim-blaming.

This defence is most likely to be used in two situations. First, some defendants may use it in situations where their interpretation of the victim's sexual reputation with other men implies that she is a willing participant. In this situation, use of this defence is unacceptable and should never be permitted. The second situation where this defence is likely to be used involves those situations in which the victim and the offender have had a prior sexual relationship: husbands and lovers.

In these two situations, the law compounds the problem associated with the honest-but-mistaken defence by allowing accused persons, who have had prior sexual relations with the victim, an unlimited right to introduce evidence relating to their prior sexual contact. In circumstances where the defence is allowed to introduce this evidence for the purpose of challenging the credibility of the victim it is a clear case of victim blaming. The victim is held accountable because she may have said yes in prior, similar circumstances. This denies her the right to have said no on the occasion for which the accused is charged.

Rape mythology has long portrayed women as not saying what they mean in sexual foreplay. Within this stereotype women are expected to resist men's initial sexual overtures, but are also expected to give in to persistent male demands. Men are expected not to take the initial no as a final answer. Because the honest-but-mistaken defence serves to perpetuate this myth, the ideal solution would be to prohibit this defence in all rape and sexual assault cases.

However, given that abolition is likely to meet with strong opposition, a more immediately achievable objective is restricting its use. The defence should be allowed only in circumstances where the victim's behaviour on the occasion for which the offender stands accused can be shown to have given the offender the impression of consent. No sexual history between the accused and the victim, or between anyone else and the victim, should be permitted. It is the behaviour of the victim and the accused on the occasion for which the accused is charged that is in question. No prior events should be allowed to be examined. If the defence is allowed to exclude evidence of prior rapes or sexual assaults on the grounds that only behaviour during the incident in question should be allowed to determine guilt or innocence, the victim should be granted the same protection. Given the power imbalances that have existed and continue to exist between men and women, this is the only appropriate solution.

Changes in Police Processing of Rape and Sexual Assault

While changes in the way rape and sexual assault cases are handled at all levels of the criminal justice system are needed, our concern here are the ways in which police processing needs to be changed. A major problem with police enforcement practices is the tendency to dismiss complaints from certain types of women (Clark and Lewis, 1977; Hinch, 1988a, 1988b). There is no doubt that some incidents reported to the police are instances where no sexual assault has taken place, or where insufficient evidence exists to make good court referrals. Nevertheless, it is doubtful that all such cases are unfounded, and that the percentage of unfounded cases is as high as indicated in official statistics.

It is more reasonable to deal with these cases in a manner other than declaring them unfounded. That is why Clark and Lewis (1977) call for the use of the term unfounded/possibly founded. They suggest that this term be used whenever the evidence is inconclusive. However, this classification is awkward because retention of the word unfounded continues to imply the possibility, without sufficient evidence, that the complaint could be unfounded. An alternative solution is to treat all such cases as still under investigation. Unless there is concrete evidence to suggest that a particular complainant is unfounded it should not be classified or implied to be unfounded.

Research also shows that the police, in the process of their investigations use techniques and procedures that place the victim at a disadvantage. One of these procedures is the use of the polygraph test, another is the use of medical examinations.

The 1983 Criminal Code amendments abolished the requirement that corroborative evidence be established before laying a charge of sexual assault. This was done in order to acknowledge that corroborative evidence is not always available, and that the victim's account of the event, if believed, could constitute sufficient evidence for conviction. It seems, however, that the police remain anxious about cases where they have only the contradictory statements of the accused and the victim. As a substitute for corroborative evidence, they use the polygraph test—also known as the lie detector test. The police generally use polygraphy to determine if suspects are lying.[11] Rape and sexual assault cases appear to be among the few, if not the only, cases where polygraphy is used to determine the truthfulness of victim statements. If the results of the victim's test indicates that she is experiencing tension when answering questions, the police assume she is lying.

When the police use polygraphy in rape and sexual assault cases to test the truthfulness of victim statements, their investigation is usually terminated if the victim either refuses or "fails" the test. That is, as is the case when police request suspects to submit to the polygraph, the police assume that victims who refuse or fail a polygraph are necessarily lying. The inescapable conclusion is that polygraphy is used in rape and sexual assault cases as a mechanism for weeding out, rather than including cases for court referral.

The solution to this problem lies in banning the use of the polygraph in all rape and sexual assault cases. The polygraph is nothing more than a device for determining stress when answering questions. It is well known that rape and sexual assault victims experience stress as a consequence of being assaulted. When a victim is asked to take a lie detector test it is a clear implication that the police believe she is lying. This only adds to the stress she is experiencing, and may, therefore, distort the results of the test.

Similarly, medical examinations and tests used to verify allegations of penetration are also used to weed out, rather than to include cases for court referral (Hinch, 1988b). Despite the fact that the current law does not require proof of penetration, medical tests, although unnecessary, are used to corroborate the victim's allegation of penetration. Where

---

[11] In his discussion of research on the use of polygraphy by police, Brannigan (1984) notes that accused who refuse to take the test are usually assumed by the police to be guilty, and that confessions are obtained in 50 to 70 percent of cases where polygraphy is used.

proof of penetration is not obtained through these tests, there is a tendency to discontinue police investigations.

If the current laws regarding corroborative evidence are to have any meaning, and if there is no need to prove penetration, why are medical examinations a routine procedure in all instances where penetration is alleged? Despite what may be considered the good intentions of the police and the medical profession to provide corroborative evidence, the lack of corroboration is detrimental to the victim's case. If under the current law, corroboration is not required, and there is sufficient additional evidence that a sexual assault did occur, it is appropriate to proceed on the available evidence rather than terminate the investigation with the implication that the victim is lying. Even if the law is changed in the manner previously suggested, it still seems preferable to proceed on the basis that the victim's statements are credible or that at least a sexual assault has occurred.

Police decision making is also based on their court experiences. The kinds of biases displayed by police in their decision making are also displayed at other points in the criminal justice system. Gunn and Minch (1988) report that decisions of crown prosecutors differ in no significant way from police decisions. They report that the only cases terminated by crown prosecutors were those left unclassified by the police.[12] This may be attributed to both an indication that the police are good at second guessing what prosecutors will do, and a high degree of convergence between police and crown prosecutors on what makes a good case. The good case features women without tarnished social reputations, as well as cases where abundant corroborative evidence exists. Studies of court decision making also indicate that the biases displayed by the police also influence court decisions (Barrett and Marshall, 1990; Ellis, 1986; Feild and Bienen, 1980).

Substantial changes are needed throughout the criminal justice system. As Gunn and Minch argue (1988: 136–137):

---

[12] Gunn and Minch (1988) also indicate that, while crown prosecutors may not terminate cases referred to them by the police, they may either reduce charges or add charges. In both cases, this is done to increase the probability of conviction. The decision may be made that there is insufficient evidence for conviction on the major charge, so a reduced charge is entered. In some instances, charges may be reduced in exchange for a guilty plea from the offender. Where charges are added, the crown may still seek conviction on the major charge, but will want to have a back up charge in case the major charge does not result in conviction. There may be sufficient evidence for a conviction on the back up charge. Curiously, Gunn and Minch found no evidence to support the assumption that laying additional charges resulted in higher probability of conviction.

The notion of breaking down the old structures and re-establishing new institutions devoid of discrimination is an overwhelming concept. Yet, it would appear that, given the imbalance of male/female power, this idea is the only answer.

If sensitivity training is needed as a means for teaching men how not to be aggressive and domineering, it is logical to assume that police investigators should also undergo such retraining. Police have a job to do which may not always be a pleasant; however, there is no reason why their job has to make victims' lives any more unpleasant than they are as a result of their victimization.

Summary

This chapter concentrated on the biases and mythology that surround rape and sexual assault. It has shown how some cultural biases have been incorporated into sociological theories of rape and sexual assault. Most importantly, suggestions have been made for changing the way the criminal justice system handles complaints, as well as changes in how the law and men conceive of rape and sexual assault.

To answer to the question "How much rape and sexual assault is there in Canada?", it is necessary to define what is meant by these terms and to decide on how to gather the evidence. If rape and sexual assault are broadly defined, then more incidents may be termed rape or sexual assault. If they are narrowly defined, fewer acts may be counted. This chapter has opted for broad definitions. Rape refers to unconsented acts of penetration of the vagina, anus or mouth for the purpose of committing a sexual act. This allows recognition of both heterosexual and homosexual rape. Sexual assault is defined as any unconsented sexual touching.

Using a broad definition of rape it is obvious that there is more rape than is revealed in Table 4–1. It does not include homosexual rape as rape, and it does not include as rape those incidents in which female victims were penetrated by objects other than a penis. Also missing are incidents of forced oral sex as rape. Furthermore, the rape rates presented in Table 4–1 do not include events that go unreported to the police. Evidence exists showing that somewhere between 60 and 90 percent of rapes go unreported.

Similarly, using a broad definition of sexual assault, and the knowledge that not all events are reported to the police, it is evident that the rate of sexual assault is higher than the rates indicated in Tables 4–1 and 4–2. The type of rape and sexual assault incidents that go unreported to the police include incidents in which the victim and offender have a close relationship, as well as incidents in which the victim simply does not wish to make known his or her victimization.

Regardless of the definitions, it is obvious that much needs to be done, and can be done to reduce the amount of rape and sexual assault, as well as improve victim confidence in the criminal justice system. The legal definitions of rape and sexual assault need to be changed to satisfy the need for gender neutral terminology, as well as reflect the seriousness of the events being defined. The law, the police and court processing of complaints need to improve in order to reduce the tendency for victim blaming. Men need to become aware that there are ways in which they can reduce the rate of sexual violence even if they believe they are unlikely to be engage in such activity. Men need to know that they must contribute as much as women to the develop of a non-sexist society, and that such a society can not be developed without their willingness to take action.

5

CORPORATE VIOLENCE

Most research on violence examines crimes, such as murder, rape, child abuse, and riots. Corporate violence is often ignored. However, this problem, in the form of pollution, unsafe products and hazardous working conditions, results in far more death and injury than does conventional criminal violence (Reasons et al., 1981; Simon and Eitzen, 1986). For example, in the U.S., one blue collar worker in four dies from cancer resulting from exposure to toxic substances at work, and almost 30,000 people die each year from using unsafe consumer products (Frank, 1985). In Canada, Reasons, et al., (1981: 28) found that Canadians are 28 times more likely to be the victims of workplace violence than they are to be victims of conventional criminal assaults. Canadians are 18 times more likely to die on the job than they are to be murdered. Reasons et al. also note that one out of every ten Canadians becomes ill or is injured on the job. These totals exclude deaths or injuries caused by both the use of unsafe products and exposure to air and water pollution.

Moreover, these statistics do not differentiate between injury and death rates for men and women. Corporate violence is yet another area in which the problems women encounter are either assumed to be the same as those encountered by men, or to be less important because there are too few women to count.[1]

---

[1] The phrase "too few to count" is included in the title of Adelberg and Currie's (1987) book on female criminal offenders. The title refers to the sometimes implicit, often explicit, assumption that there are not enough female criminals to warrant paying attention to female crime. Adelberg and Currie correctly assert that the assumption is unwarranted. Similarly, our use of this phrase in reference to the number of female victims of workplace violence implies that there is good reason to study the nature and types of corporate violence against women.

What Is Corporate Violence?

There is much disagreement in the white collar and corporate crime literature about whether or not the behaviour being analyzed is crime. For some, behaviour can not be considered crime unless it is a direct violation of criminal law (see Tappan, 1947). For others, any behaviour assessed as illegal by a court, including civil court, regulatory commission or other quasi judicial body should be defined as crime (Sutherland, 1940, 1945). These acts must be treated for analytical purposes as crime because they all represent instances of illegal conduct, and it is the sociologist's/criminologist's job to understand illegal conduct of all kinds. Still others argue that it is important to recognize that some wrongdoings are not illegal. Corporate executives, or others acting on behalf of corporations, may not be committing illegal acts. However, these acts cause far more harm than those actions labelled criminal by the courts and the law. These actions are not labelled criminal because certain powerful interests are able to influence the creation of the law to ensure that their behaviour patterns are not criminalized (Goff and Reasons, 1978; Pearce, 1973; Simon and Eitzen, 1986).

Most of the literature on corporate illegality argues that it should be treated as criminal behaviour (Coleman, 1985; Goff and Reasons, 1978; Reasons et al., 1981; Simon and Eitzen, 1986). According to Reasons et al. (1981: 9), a conventionally defined criminal assault occurs " ... when a person either applies force intentionally to another person or, by an act or gesture, causes another person to have reasonable grounds to believe that there will be an interference with his or her physical integrity." Arguing that acts of corporate violence should also be considered criminal is simply an extension of the same legal principle. The assaultive behaviour of corporations, corporate executives, or other agents of the corporation does not differ significantly from conventionally defined criminal assaults.

Criminal law has, of course, been applied in the past to acts of corporate violence. However, it has been applied infrequently, and sometimes illogically. For example, in 1987, a mineworker in Sudbury, Ontario, was charged with criminal negligence causing death in the deaths of four co-workers (Michaud, 1988). The mineworker turned off an air valve which allowed a gate to open sending tons of water and crushed rock down a mine shaft burying the four men. He was not advised by his employer or his supervisors that an important bypass airline had been inoperable for more than 10 months. His supervisors, and the company he worked for (Inco) both knew about the faulty air valve but were charged with lessor offences under the *Occupational Health and Safety Act of Ontario*. It matters little that the mineworker in this case was subsequently acquitted in criminal court of any wrongdoing, and that the employer was fined $60,000. What matters is that the worker, who did not know that the air value was faulty, faced criminal prosecution while his supervisor and employer, who knew about the faulty valve, faced non-criminal charges. He was doing his job as required by his employer, but he was doing it without vital information in the control of his supervisors and his employer. This is a clear case of the wrongful use of criminal courts in enforcing safety on the job.

What is needed, therefore, is a reorganization of the law. Violations of occupational health and safety law, as well as violations of consumer law, especially where these involve danger to health or safety, must be recognized as criminal violations. Corporate violence should face the same potential for criminal prosecution as does conventionally defined criminal violence. Corporations, executives, and other agents of the corporation can not be allowed to escape criminal prosecution. Common law tradition has long been extended to cover prosecution of the corporation, its officers and agents (Coleman, 1985). Logically, of course, a corporation is just a legal fiction. As a legal person it exists only on paper. To allow executives to escape punishment by prosecuting only the corporation is an act of class bias. Consequently, whenever the legal fiction is charged, its officers or agents who planned or carried out the action, or who failed to prevent or reduce danger, should also be held criminally responsible.

But is it violence? Many people are reluctant to call certain actions violent if the victim and the offender do not meet in a face-to-face encounter, or if the offence is one in which the offender did not target a specific victim. Many acts of corporate violence to be discussed in this chapter do not involve face-to-face encounters and do not involve the targeting of specific victims. Why, then, are they presented along with acts of face-to-face violence and instances of victim targeting as incidents of corporate violence?

The short answer to this question is that even though victim and offender do not meet, and the offender may not target a specific person, the offender's actions are usually planned. The offender knows that his or her behaviour will threaten someone's health or safety. As Reasons, et al., (1981: 7) point out:

> The violation of safety and health standards and/or the failure to establish adequate standards is usually a rational, premeditated, conscious choice concerning capital expenses and business profits.

These rational, premeditated, conscious choices endanger real people.

Corporate violence is any behaviour undertaken in the name of the corporation by decision makers, or other persons in authority within the corporation, that endangers the health or safety of employees or other persons who are affected by that behaviour. Even acts of omission, in which decision makers, etc., refuse to take action to reduce or eliminate known health and safety risks, must be considered corporate violence. It is the impact the action has on the victim, not the intent of the act, which determines whether or not it is violence.

How Many Women Are Victims of Corporate Violence?

It is difficult to answer the above question because there is a lack of data. Job injury rates are collected primarily by pooling male and female injuries. Consequently, this chapter centres on types of injury and illness rather than the number of incidents. The following discussion is divided into two sections. The first deals with violence on the job. The second addresses the manufacture, sale and distribution of unsafe products.

Workplace Violence

The myth that women's health and safety issues are not as significant as men's health and safety issues is based on two interrelated, faulty assumptions. First, it assumes that, because fewer women than men are employed in the paid labour force, women are not exposed to workplace violence. Second, it assumes that, because few women work in so called heavy industry, such as mining, steel, and logging, women do not encounter workplace hazards.

The first of these two assumptions is easily dismissed. There are significantly more women in the paid labour force now than in the past 100 years. In 1891, women comprised 11 percent of the total labour force. By 1988, women made up 44 percent of the labour force. Furthermore, the rate at which women are entering the labour force is increasing. Whereas 35 percent of women worked outside the home in 1966, 48 percent were in the paid labour force by 1978, and 53 percent were working by 1988. These are not insignificant numbers. Thus, to assume that there are too few working women to worry about the health and safety risks to which they are exposed is to ignore the reality.

Turning to the second assumption, clearly, there are more women working in traditionally male dominated industries today than there has been in several decades. Consequently, more women are exposed to the dangers of these workplaces. But this apparent surge in the number of women working in traditionally male occupations really represents some women's return to some of these industries. During the first half of the 1800s, women were employed in occupations and industries now seen as male occupations and industries.

Women disappeared from these industries not because they were unable, or unwilling to do the job, but because they were forced out by legislators, employers, and even male co-workers. These people thought that the above work was both unfeminine and undesirable for women (Johnson, 1974; Zaretsky, 1976). At the same time, advancing industrial technology also paved the way for employers to use fewer employees. Thus, the mythology that women work in less dangerous occupations than men began to take shape during an era in which women were forced out of the workplace by advancing technology and by clearly ideological factors.

Furthermore, in this century, many women worked in heavy industry. During both world wars, women did the dangerous work needed to produce not only the machinery of war, but the other vital materials needed to sustain the economy (Ramkhalawansing, 1974). There were even some studies during WWII which attempted to ascertain the health and safety risks to which female workers were exposed as a result of entry into male occupations (Baetjer, 1977).

However, it is dishonest to suggest that either the simple increase in the number of working women, or the number of women working in heavy industries are sufficient reasons to re-evaluate the dangers women face in the workplace. Whether or not there are more working women, or whether women work in the same occupations as men, women encounter hazardous working conditions. Thus, while 73 percent of working women in 1988 (Parliament, 1990) still worked in traditional female ghettos (clerical, sales or service industries, as well as teaching or health services), this does not mean that they work in safe occupations. It is not necessary for women to work in the same occupations as men in order to be exposed to dangerous situations or to experience the ill effects of exposure to toxic substances, stress, etc. Working women have been, and still are, exposed to a wide variety of occupational health and safety hazards.

In detailing the types of health and safety risks to which working women are exposed, our discussion is divided into two sections: the hazards of working in industrial settings, and the hazards of office, clerical work and service sector work.

Danger in Industrial Work

The specific hazards encountered by female industrial workers are shown in Table 5-1.[2] Note that virtually all types of work pose some hazard. Of particular interest is the number of women who face the threat of damage to their reproductive health, including damage to fetuses and children because of exposure to toxic substances during pregnancy. Women in all occupations seem to face these hazards.

This is not a relatively new problem. For example, the hazardous effects of lead exposure on pregnant women was well established in Europe during the 19th century. By 1919, most European countries restricted women's access to jobs which involved exposure to lead (Klein, 1987). What is, perhaps, surprising is that the battle to reduce the risks of exposure is still being waged.

An even more worrisome problem is the use of chemicals with effects on humans that are not yet known. The hazards of some of chemical substances, such as benzine, is well known; however, many other chemical hazards have yet to be identified. Since the dangerous effects of these new substances are unknown, manufacturers are not required to advise consumers of potential dangers, and workers are being exposed to unknown hazards.

Exposure to toxic substances, however, is not the only health and safety issue facing contemporary working women. As indicated in Table 5-1, women working in industrial settings encounter stress, both mental and physical. Whether it is the product of poor ventilation, the work pace, or the often dehumanizing situations in which women must do their jobs, stress can lead to severe problems, such as heart disease, hypertension, ulcers, etc.

Armstrong (1984) and Rinehart (1987) show that much of the stress comes from the use of machinery that is designed for reasons other than increasing the job satisfaction of the worker using that equipment. These machines are designed to satisfy management needs, such as increased efficiency and management control of the work process. People who must work at the pace set by the machine perceive a loss of control over their work. This increases job stress.

For example, food processing plants require employees to perform a number of tasks in quick succession while using either sharp knives, or saws for cutting through bones. This increases the risk of injury, in the form of burns (from hot ovens, burners, etc.), scalds (from hot water),

---

[2] This table is adapted from research presented by Reasons et al. (1981) and Chenier (1982).

and cuts (from knives or saws). The risk of stress is also increased. Armstrong and Armstrong (1983: 128) provide the following example:

> Basically, I stand there all day and slash the necks of the chickens. You make one slash up on the skin of the neck and then you cut around the base of the neck so the person beside you can crop it ... The chickens go in front of you on the line and you do every other chicken or whatever. And you stand their for eight hours on one spot and do it.

The pace at which the chickens are delivered to each worker is determined by assessments of the time it takes to perform each movement. A computer then regulates the conveyer belt. At one poultry processing plant, chickens are moved along the line at a rate of 58 per minute, or 3,480 birds an hour (Shartal, 1988: 8). This requires individual meat cutters to make 87 separate body movements, including arm and back movements, each minute, or 5,220 movements an hour. The speed of the line, and the required number of movements contribute to both mental and physical stress. The mental stress increases the potential for physical problems such as ulcers, while the physical stress increases the potential for repetitive strain injuries (RSI) to the back and upper limbs.

An additional source of stress for many female workers, and one to which men are typically not exposed is sexual harassment. Sexual harassment, as defined by Fonow (1983), is unsolicited, unreciprocated male behaviour that values a woman's sex role over her function as a worker. It includes a wide range of actions. Some examples are, persistent propositions for dates, suggestions that decisions to hire or promote are dependent on provision of sexual favours, acts of sexual touching including rape, the threat to transfer or the actual transfer of a worker to a more difficult job if sexual favours are not provided, dirty jokes, verbal threats to perform unwanted sexual acts, and repeated references to either the woman's sexuality or the sexual urges of male co-workers. Women may be harassed by employers, supervisors or co-workers.

Many of these actions can be processed as criminal events, especially any threatened or actual acts of unconsented sexual touching, as well as an employer's demand for sexual favours in exchange for job security or promotion. However, they are typically, processed through grievance procedures or through civil and human rights procedures.

Sexual harassment is often made worse in situations where supervisors or employers know of its existence but refuse to take action to stop it. "Selective inattention" (Dexter, 1958) to sexual harassment is often based on the assumption that it is harmless, or humorous, or even flattering. In reality, female victims suffer both physical and mental health

TABLE 5-1: Hazards—Industrial and Other Work Sites

HAZARD	WORKERS AT RISK	PROBLEM CAUSED
asbestos (brake linings, insulation, some textiles)	auto workers, textile workers, insulation workers, anyone working near exposed asbestos fibres	cancer (asbestosis)
fatigue (caused by changes in hours of work, stress, noise, loss of sleep)	shift workers	changes in menstrual cycle, body temperature, blood pressure, liver and kidney funtion
benzene (in solvents and cleaners)	workers producing or using solvents, plastics, rubbers, glues, dyes, detergents, paints, and petroleum	prolonged menstrual bleeding, postpartum haemorrhaging, birth defects, children have higher rates of leukemia and illnesses from contaminated milk
beryllium	ceramic workers, electonics workers, jewelry makers, lab workers, nuclear technologists	during pregnancy beryllium poisoning may cause death, fetus may also be affected
lead	auto workers, ceramic and pottery workers, electronics workers, farmers, pesticide workers, paint makers, paint users, typographers	infertility, miscarriages, stillbirths, menstrual disorders, neonatal death, mental retardation among children of women exposed to lead or lead products
radiation, anesthetics and mercury vapours	dentists, dental assistants & nurses, hygienists	liver disease, central nervous system changes, fetal damage (even the wives of male dentists may risk spontaneous abortions)
mercury	dentists, dental workers, battery makers, farm workers, jewelry makers, lithographers, pesticide makers, photographic chemical makers and users	miscarriages, stillbirths, as well as fetal brain damage and mental retardation
pesticides, insecticides, fungicides	farmers, farm wives, farm workers	allergies, bacterial and viral infections, lung diseases, skin cancer, miscarriages, chromosone changes, birth deformities

Hazard	Workers affected	Effects
hormones including DES	pharmaceutical workers, lab workers, farmers and veterinarians	irregular menstruation, infertility, ovarium cysts, breast lumps, cancer of reproductive system, fetuses may develop signs of sexual maturity, such as enlarged breasts, DES may cause cancer in female children and genital abnormalities in male children
sexual harassment (from male co-workers, bosses, etc.)	all female workers	stress, stress related illnesses such as ulcers
vinyl chloride	workers producing vinyl chloride and polyviral chloride and products using these	genetic damage to ovum, stillbirths/fetal death, birth defects, fetuses may develop cancer, miscarriages
anesthetic gases, radiation, contagious stress and mental pressure	hospital employees (nurses, doctors, lab tachnicians, cleaning and laundry workers, cooks, dieticians and physiotherapists)	spontaneous abortion, congenital abnormalities in children
lint, dust	textile workers, agricultural workers, dry cleaners, cancer, various allergic reactions	
heat, or heat and humidity	garment and textile workers	heat exhaustion, heat stress, fatigue, irritability, and susceptibility to accidents
poor ventilation (areas at greatest distance from windows air conditioners)	all workers	stress (physical and mental) heart disease, ulcers, hypertension, pneumontis (a disease caused by build up of bacteria in the cooling fluids of air conditioners which are then distributed throughout a building)
repetitive wrist, arm and back movements	assembly line workers, food processing workers	muscle strain, tensoynovitis, other repetitive strain injuries

problems. Some women are unable to do their jobs effectively. Consequently, they could be dismissed from their jobs, or the may decide to quit their jobs rather than risk further harassment. Moreover, as articulated in Figure 5-1 on page 128[3], sexual harassment may even threaten someone's life.

In the case described in Figure 5-1, the victim quit her job, sought psychiatric help, and even attempted suicide because she thought her situation was hopeless. Her supervisors and employer refused to take action to stop the harassment she received from her male co-workers. As in this case, victims are often blamed for provoking harassment. Employers who refuse to take action become accomplices.

A significant problem contributing to injury rates is lack of training. Reasons et al., (1981) and Simon and Eitzen (1986) note that many workers are placed in dangerous jobs without being trained to do them, or without being advised of the risks involved. The Karen Silkwood case, and the asbestos industry's attempt to cover up the harmful effects of asbestos, are two of the best examples of employers refusing to tell workers about the dangers of working with toxic substances. In the Silkwood case, plutonium workers were provided with little or no training in the handling of plutonium, and were not told of its potential to cause cancer.

In the asbestos case, employers hid the ill effects of asbestos since the 1930s. Even though insurance companies began as early as 1919 to refuse to insure asbestos workers, and the companies were in possession of clear evidence of the harmful effects of asbestos, asbestos companies denied and covered up information showing that exposure to asbestos caused asbestosis. They even paid for research that showed that asbestos was not harmful.

Thus, while it is common for employers and provincial workers' Compensation Boards to blame the worker for their injuries, many occupational diseases and accidents are caused by conditions within the employer's control (Reasons et al., 1981). Through such measures as better and more frequent safety inspections, as well as better training of employees who must work with dangerous machinery, or chemicals, or in dangerous situations, Reasons et al. argue that job injuries and illnesses can be significantly reduced.

Only a small number of women working in so called unskilled jobs, such as those in the food processing industry, had any training which prepared them for their jobs (Armstrong and Armstrong, 1983). Women

---

[3]   This article was written by Leslie Papp (1990: A1, A20) for the *Toronto Star.*

who work in food processing plants are assumed to be already familiar with the technology of food preparation. Unskilled jobs, such as packing boxes on an assembly line, are also assumed to require little, if any, training. The little training that is provided may consist of only a few minutes of instruction from another worker. The worker is shown how to do the job quickly and efficiently. Little or no time is spent on safety training. Moreover, Reasons et al. (1981) note employers often require work to be done at a pace that forces even skilled and trained workers to abandon use of safety equipment. The consequence is higher injury rates and condemnation of the workers for failing to use safe procedures.

Office, Clerical and Service Sector Hazards

At first glance the notion that office, clerical and service sector work is dangerous seems ludicrous. There is no heavy machinery, no risk of losing a hand, arm or leg in the machinery, and none of the risks associated with mining, fishing and logging, the most dangerous areas in which men work. It is assumed that office and clerical work does not involve lifting of heavy objects or exposure to toxic substances. A closer examination reveals a somewhat different picture.

Table 5-2[4] shows that office and clerical workers face many of same hazards as other workers. Of course, female workers are not the only workers exposed to these hazards.[5] The point, however, is not that female clerical workers encounter these hazards with more or less frequency than male workers. The point is that clerical workers face these hazards, and, consequently, their workplaces are hazardous. The specific hazards range from noise, to stress, to exposure to dangerous tools (knives for example), to exposure to various toxic substances, to problems associated with lighting, to sexual harassment. Even the seemingly harmless act of sitting can lead to health problems.

Some hazards are less serious than others. Nevertheless, even some of the seemingly less harmful problems can have devastating consequences. Female workers earning their living by making repetitive wrist, arm and back movements, such as secretaries, and other keyboard workers, face the possibility of repetitive strain injuries such as tendonitis and carpal tunnel syndrome (CPS). CPS is a painful condition caused

---

[4] This table is adapted from research reported by Reasons et al., (1981) and Chenier (1982).

[5] For example, male workers exposed to stress, noise, poor ventilation and solvents, or other chemicals, face similar risks of sterility, heart disease and cancer.

TABLE 5-2: Hazards—Office, Clerical and Service Sector

HAZARD	WORKERS AT RISK	PROBLEM CAUSED
radiation (from VDTs--video display terminals-- and various other sources including x-rays)	dental and chiropractor office workers, hospital employees	sterility (male and female), premature aging of sex cells, damage to fetus including prenatal death, mental retardation, birth defects, leukemia and cancer
poor ventilation (areas at greatest distance from windows air conditioners)	all workers	stress (physical and mental) heart disease, ulcers, hypertension, pneumontis (a disease caused by build up of bacteria in the cooling fluids of air conditioners which are then distributed throughout a building)
noise (from office machinery including typewriters, copiers and printers)	typists, photo copier operators	stress hypertension
poor lighting (old style fluorescent)	all office workers exposed to this light source	has been associated with hypertension in children
ozone and other gases (from photo copiers, carpets, paints, plastics)	photo copier operators, all office workers	eye, nose and throat irritations, cancer
asbestos (insulation, some textiles)	anyone working near exposed asbestos fibres	cancer (asbestosis)
repetitive wrist and arm movements	typists, cashiers, VDT operators	muscle strain, tensoynovitis, carpal tunnel syndrome (a disabling wrist disorder)
prolonged sitting	typists, receptionists and other workers who sit most of the working day	backstrain, may impede circulation
solvents, and other chemicals (in cleaners, glues, mimeograph machines, benzene based products, photocopiers)	cleaners, mimeograph operators, and photo copier operators, or anyone using these products	skin, eye, nose and throat irritations: benzene linked to leukemia and genetic defects, chromosome changes, and prolonged menstrual bleeding, as well as postpartum haemorrhage

hair sprays, hair tonics, soaps, detergents, perfumes, nail polish, dyes	hairdressers	bacterial infections, skin irritations, cancer, liver and bladder ailments, respiratory diseases
anesthetic gases, radiation, contagious stress and mental pressure	hospital employees (nurses, doctors, lab technicians, cleaning and laundry workers, cooks, dieticians and physiotherapists)	spontaneous abortion, congenital abnormalities in children
sexual harassment (fom male co-workers, bosses, etc.)	all female workers	stress, stress related illnesses such as ulcers
stress (from on the job pressure to perform)	all office/clerical workers	coronary heart disease, ulcers, hypertension
fatigue (caused by changes in climate and stress, noise, loss of sleep)	flight attendents, and shift workers	changes in menstrual cycle, body temperature, blood pressure, liver and kidney function
contact with children	teachers, child care workers	stress, ulcers, hypertension, contagious diseases
hot stoves, burns, hot water, and knives	all food service workers (cooks, food servers)	burns, scalding, cuts

by repeated, rapid hand and wrist movement producing swelling in the wrists which pinches the nerves. Many women with these two conditions are unable to continue working. Armstrong and Armstrong (1983) provide other examples of hazards: haemorrhoids (secretaries or other workers who spend long days sitting), back pain (secretaries, telephone operators, etc., who must sit on chairs that give inadequate support to the back), circulation problems (resulting from standing or sitting long hours in one place).

Food service workers, including cooks and waitresses or other food servers, face many of the same hazards as food processing workers. They work with hot stoves, hot grease and oil that can burn, sharp knives that cut easily, and boiling water that can burn or scald. Like food processing workers, they are rarely trained to use their equipment. Employers assume that workers know how to use it safely. Sometimes employees work in cramped, poorly designed work stations with little or no first aid training or inappropriate first aid kits.

For example, a medium sized Canadian university (approximately 11,000 students) recently opened a lunch counter in one of its academic buildings.[6] This space was designed to be self-serve, with two arrays of 8 burners each for coffee, a cooler for milk, juices and sandwiches, a display of chocolate bars, gum and other candy, a cold drink dispenser, and a cash register. Except during rush hours, a single worker is responsible for making sure that the coffee pots are full, the shelves of sandwiches and other products are properly stocked, and for tending the cash register. However, the space was not designed to provide easy access to the storage space. In addition to storage areas under the counters, where the burners are located, two storage shelves are located about eight feet above and behind the burners. To gain access to the shelves, workers must climb a small ladder (approximately two feet high), and then stand on the counter beside one of the burners. On one occasion, while attempting to gain access to the storage shelves a lone female worker accidently placed her hand on one of the burners. She received first degree burns to her thumb and two fingers, and second degree burns to two other fingers. Some of her skin was burned onto the burner. She telephoned her supervisor, who worked in another building, while holding her hand under the cold water tap and continuing to wait on customers. After receiving medical attention, she returned

---

[6] The incident reported here was witnessed by one of the authors in November, 1990.

to the job less than two hours later. She claimed that similar accidents are an almost daily occurrence at the university.

While it is easy to blame her for not checking to see if the burner was on, the real problem here is the location of the storage shelves. They are located where they create a high risk of injury. It is a type of injury to which food service workers are constantly exposed. Sometimes, as in this case, the injuries are not severe. At other times, the injuries are more serious. Workers may not be able to return to work, and that means lost income. Even when people are covered by Workers' Compensation, they may be without an income for a prolonged period between the injury and the receipt of compensation, and the compensation never equals the workers' full pay.

This places workers under even more stress. They and their families are dependent not only on the income, but on receiving that income at regular intervals. Groceries must be purchased, and landlords, mortgage companies, and other creditors, want their money when it is due. The prolonged delays in receiving Workers' Compensation payments means angry landlords and/or creditors. The reduced income, when it comes, also means that there is less money to pay the bills.

It is also obvious that clerical workers are not immune to the hazards posed by exposure to toxic substances. Like workers in industrial settings, clerical staff are exposed to an increasing number of toxic substances. For example, the use of office machinery, such as photo copiers, requires the use of various toxic substances: printing powders or fluids, etc. Similarly, exposure to asbestos, used to insulate heating pipes, etc., is not confined to industrial workers. Where asbestos remains in use, there is always potential for exposure. That is why asbestos products are used less frequently today than they were in the past. It is also the reason why strict guidelines are in place for its removal in instances where the protective coverings surrounding it have deteriorated to the point where fibres are released into the air.

The full extent of the risk, however, is not known. Experts are divided on the amount of exposure deemed acceptable. As in other instances where exposure levels are regulated by law, exposure to radiation for example, government guidelines have been criticized for allowing too much exposure. In general terms, the introduction of toxic substances into the office means more and more office workers risk cancer, respiratory illness, and/or risks to their reproductive health (Chenier, 1982).

Manufacturers of toxic substances claim that their products are safe if used according to their instructions, and if proper training is provided. The problem is that the employers of office workers, like the employers of factory workers, do not always provide training. Consequently, accidents happen, spills occur, and workers' health is put at risk.

Further, the gases emitted from petro-chemical based products, including carpeting, office furniture, paint, etc., contribute to overall exposure levels. This is especially true in sealed buildings dependent on air conditioning systems for ventilation. Ventilation systems do not always function properly, or are poorly designed, and thus do not necessarily permit sufficient fresh air to be circulated throughout the building. When this happens, harmful gases build up that may lead in the short-term to headaches and fainting. In the long- term, it may lead to any of a variety of problems associated with the type of gases and vapours that build up. The term sick building is used to refer to sealed buildings with inadequate fresh air and a buildup of hazardous gases.

Clerical work does not exempt women from injuries caused from lifting or moving heavy objects. Clerical personnel and sales clerks are often required to move heavy boxes. For example:

> 'I can remember carrying a box that was so heavy that I had to kick it along the floor.' This secretary regularly carts around stacks of printed material, lugging it up and down the stairs. A sales clerk does the same thing with boxes of candy that weigh as much as 25 pounds. One clerical worker who was having difficulty moving a heavy parcel asked the professional she works for to help her. He said he would do it only if it was clear that he would get compensation if he hurt his back (Armstrong and Armstrong, 1983: 186)!

Even cashiers at grocery stores are required to lift from 3,500 to 17,000 pounds of food and other items during an eight hour shift (Shartal, 1988). The lifting, and the twisting and turning of the back in order to do the lifting result in back strain that is often sufficient to cause lost time on the job, or even permanent disability. Shartal also contends that the weight and twisting and turning required results in 40 percent of cashiers suffering at least one repetitive strain injury in their lifetimes.

As in other settings, one of the more difficult health and safety issues women encounter is the failure of employers to take complaints of ill health seriously. As Armstrong and Armstrong (1983: 193) point out, even when women are obviously ill their employers may not allow them to take time off work:

> Even when I was proofreading, I had a strep throat. I told ... my supervisor. She called me back because ... the boss told her to ask me if I could move my hands, could I see good, could I walk to get to work? Then come in because all he needed was for me to move the

pencil to read. I didn't go in. But imagine! And this has been done to several people on that job. No compassion shown at all there. None at all.

In this case the woman did not give in to the pressure to go to work while ill. In many other cases, women submit to the pressure to work while ill or injured. The pressure takes different forms, including threats of job loss and loss of income. Consequently, not only is women's health threatened, but their financial stability is threatened if they take time off from work because of illness. Even though hourly paid employees are sometimes permitted a number of "sick days" per year without fear of job loss, many are not paid for these days. To avoid income loss they work while ill. These women face either working while ill, or quitting their jobs.

In another case, an employer's failure to take a woman's complaint of sexual harassment seriously made her quit her job. She worked in the computer room of a large retailer, and complained to her supervisors that her co-workers were sexually harassing her (Gorrie, 1990). After telling her supervisors that male co-workers repeatedly used obscene language, bragged about their sexual adventures in her presence, and even stripped down to their underwear when left alone with her, she was told that she was partly to blame. She was faulted for having an outgoing personality, for getting along well with her co-workers, and for changing into jogging clothes in the women's washroom to go jogging during her lunch break. She was even told that she had to learn how to get along with her co-workers. This amounts to the same type of victim-blaming experienced by victims of sexual assault.

Office workers are also not immune to stress. The pressure to get the job done quickly and without error is a constant in all types of work situations. As in industrial settings, stress is sometimes created by the introduction of new technology into the workplace. The revolution in micro-technology, which many workers fear will replace them, creates tension. Tension also results from the way in which the technology is utilized. When used to increase productivity, it can force even the office or clerical worker to work at the pace of the machine.

A good example of what is meant here is computer hardware and software used by bank tellers, airline ticket agents, secretaries and telephone operators. Each has had to face the introduction of computer technology that enables them to process more information faster than they did previously. In each case, however, introduction of this technology lead to a decline in job satisfaction and an increase in stress.

For example, the introduction of new computer technology allowed telephone companies to increase the number of calls, as many as four each minute, and to continuously monitor the work process: to monitor each call, the duration of the call, and the total number of calls in any given time period (Bernard, 1982: Czerny and Swift, 1988). Time taken for coffee breaks, to go to the washroom, etc., can also be monitored. Prior to the introduction of this equipment, operators were able to prolong the time between calls by not responding to the switches they controlled. This allowed them to have brief conversations with other operators, or to simply take a short break. With computer monitoring, these opportunities for brief contact with sister workers declined, and so did job satisfaction.

While job satisfaction declined, the number of RSI complaints increased. The pain from these injuries is caused by various repetitive movements needed to do the job, and from the hours of sitting in one position. One telephone operator is quoted by Armstrong and Armstrong (1983: 134) as saying:

> Last week I was not getting out very many calls ... I have a sort of chronic arthritis or something in the right shoulder and my arm felt as heavy as lead that day and they came and told me and I just said, 'Well look, my arm's giving me a lot of trouble.'

Workers who do not perform within the specified standard risk loss of job satisfaction, reprimands, and/or loss of employment.

Many clerical and service sector workers go to work with the constant threat of danger. Bank tellers, similar workers in other financial institutions, sales clerks in 24-hour convenience stores and gas stations, as well as waitresses in restaurants, bars and night clubs, face potential threats from robbery and assault. For example:

> I've had one night where a bullet went between my legs. In another nightclub, it happened once that a guy grabbed me by the throat—he was actually choking me. Nobody saw me ... A customer came by and I kicked him. He saw what was happening and he threw the guy out. I was quite lucky (as cited in Armstrong and Armstrong, 1983: 188).

Bank tellers may be given instructions on what to do during an a robbery attempt, and may even be compensated for injuries suffered during a robbery, but many other workers do not get any type of help or support (Armstrong and Armstrong, 1983). Their fears of assault, including sexual assault, and murder, are grounded in stark reality.

Violence against Female Consumers

The number and variety of unsafe products sold in the market place is staggering. Consumer safety is frequently neglected in favour of corporate profit (Coleman, 1985). Coleman quotes a former president of a large auto maker on the introduction and use of safety glass in automobiles in 1919

> I am trying to protect the interest of the stockholders of General Motors and the corporation's operating position—it is not my responsibility to sell safety glass ... You can say perhaps that I am selfish, but business is selfish. We are not a charitable institution—we are trying to make a profit for our shareholders (1985: 40).

Even when it is clearly established that their product is unsafe, some corporations continue to sell it. For example, evidence exists indicating that the Ford Motor Company knew before it began marketing its 1971 to 1976 Pintos and Bobcats that the gas tanks would explode in any rear end collisions over 25 miles per hour (Coleman, 1985), but decided to market the cars anyway. Company officials later lied and denied knowing the gas tanks were defective.

In some cases, manufacturers of unsafe products falsified test results. For example, when Richardson-Merrill learned that its drug MER/29, an intended treatment for high cholesterol, caused death in test animals, it decided to falsify the records.

> One laboratory technician testified that she was ordered by a Richardson-Merrill executive to change reports on the health problems experienced by test animals and to make up data for nonexistent animals showing no harmful effects from the use of MER/29 ... The report on one study claimed that only four of eight experimental rats had died, when in fact they all did (Coleman, 1985: 44).

When the lab technician complained to her supervisor, she was told to do as the executive had ordered and to be quiet.

These, of course, are problems faced by products sold to all consumers. The focus in this section is on the ill effects of products sold exclusively, or primarily to women, or which have shown themselves to be particularly hazardous to women. The pharmaceutical industry is extensively criticized for failing to adequately test drugs intended for human use, and for marketing drugs which it knows, or has reason to believe, are unsafe (McDonnell, 1986; Coleman, 1985). In some instances, the drug companies market products in third world countries that were banned in advanced nations (Directs and Hoen, 1986; Duggan, 1986; LaCheen, 1986; Marcelis and Shiva, 1986).

Other aspects of the pharmaceutical industry's marketing practices are also questioned. Ford (1986) notes that drug manufacturers frequently fund not only the research testing of the effects of the drug, but also the journals in which the research tests are published. The journals not only publish the test results, but also advertisements pushing the drugs. In some cases, Ford found evidence that doctors were advised, by research published in a journal financed by pharmaceutical industry sources, to withhold vital information about the potential hazards of estrogen drugs used in the treatment of vaginal atrophy (thinning of the vaginal walls causing dryness). Thus, according to Ford, reliance of doctors on industry-funded research and journals is a potential danger to women. Doctors may prescribe drug treatments without knowing all of the side effects of the drug. Thus, women's health is placed in jeopardy. The types of drugs that have been found to cause health risks to women include drugs aimed at helping women manage their reproductive life, to drugs aimed at helping women cope with stress.

Drugs and Women's Reproductive Health

The pharmaceutical industry has marketed drugs to prevent and diagnose pregnancy, increase fertility, control morning sickness during pregnancy, and to induce abortions. Unfortunately, many of these drugs adversely affect women's health. For example, thalidomide, prescribed during the late 1950s and early 1960s to pregnant women as a remedy for morning sickness, was widely marketed before it was fully tested. It was also sold after it was shown to produce birth defects. Consequently, thousands of children world wide were born with severe physical deformities. Most were born with deformed hands, arms and legs.

Other hormone drugs have also received considerable attention from critics of the pharmaceutical industry (Directs and Hoen, 1986; Ford, 1986; LaCheen, 1986; Marcelis and Shiva, 1986). Drugs containing various combinations of estrogen and progesterone, sometimes separately, sometimes together, are hazardous to the workers who make them and to the women who use them. DES (diethylstilbestrol), given to prevent miscarriages, and depo-provera, used as a contraceptive, are known carcinogens. Other estrogen/progesterone or EP drugs can cause osteoporosis, and produce birth defects including defects in the heart, the circulatory system, the central nervous system, and the limbs.

In some cases, the hazards posed by these drugs were not known prior to being marketed by the pharmaceutical industry. In other cases,

the industry continues to market the drugs while in possession of evidence showing their harmful effects. This is certainly the case with all
those hormone drugs, such as DES and depo-provera, which are currently banned in most economically advanced countries, but still marketed in the Third World. This is a clear case of the pharmaceutical
industry putting profits ahead of the health of consumers.

Finally, it is no secret that many easily accessible drugs, such as alcohol, tobacco, caffeine and antihistamines are health hazards. Alcohol
leads to alcoholism and contributes to increased rates of heart disease
and cirrhosis of the liver. Used in conjunction with sedative-hypnotic
drugs (see next section) it can kill. Similarly, lung and heart disease are
risks shared by all tobacco users. Moreover, use of tobacco products
during pregnancy creates hazards for pregnant women and their babies.
Children born of smoking mothers are lighter at birth and have slower
rates of physical and mental maturity compared to children born of
non-smoking mothers (Simon and Eitzen, 1986). Women who smoke
during pregnancy also have higher risks of miscarriages, premature
births, and still births. Antihistamines, found in cold and hay fever reme-
dies, and caffeine, found in tea, coffee, coca, cola drinks, and some cold
preparations, are also suspected of causing birth defects.

Drugs and Mental Health

Mood modifying drugs are overprescribed to women (Harding, 1986).
More women than men are prescribed stress relieving drugs, and despite
the fact that women's body size is generally smaller than men's, the
average dose prescribed to women is larger than the average dose prescribed to men. Certain women, notably the elderly, are more likely than
others to be have them prescribed.

That these drugs have been and continue to be overused is shown in
the decline in the prescription rates for darvon (propoxyphene). Harding (1986) reports that, in 1977, almost 30,000 people a year were
prescribed darvon in Saskatchewan. By 1982, less than 9,000 prescrip-
tions were being written, and the number of physicians prescribing it fell
from 717 in 1978 to 383 in 1982. Harding attributes the decline to public
concern that this drug was being used irresponsibly and that many female users did not need it. However, while the use of this drug declined,
the rate of use for sedative-hypnotic drugs increased correspondingly.

The effect of prescribing drugs unnecessarily is deceptively simple.
On a societal basis it is easier to keep those suffering from stress func-
tioning than it is to do something to relieve the sources of stress. In this
context, Harding notes that more women than men live in poverty, and

that a large segment of the poor are elderly women. Poverty, of course, is associated world-wide with health problems; including stress. Therefore, prescribing mood modifying drugs provides a remedy for a symptom of poverty, without eliminating the problem.

Harding attributes the overproliferation of mood modifying drugs to an additional factor. He questions the motives of pharmacy owners in recommending that the Saskatchewan provincial drug care plan provide prescription drugs at no cost to the elderly. It is well known that the elderly frequently do not buy prescription drugs if they are unable to afford them. Because the elderly are unable to buy the drugs without this type of aid, providing free prescription drugs to the heaviest users— the elderly—allows the pharmacist to get his/her dispensing fee. It also increases sales for the pharmaceutical companies.

Other Unsafe Products

Although there is a long list of hazardous products on the market, concern here is with those which present a danger to women's health. These products include commercial variations of those encountered in the workplace, as well as feminine hygiene products.

Many of the hazardous gases, and toxic substances referred to in Tables 5-1 and 5-2 are also found in commercial products intended for home use. Even though they are not as potent as similar products used in industrial settings, they are still potent enough to cause problems.

Paints containing lead and/or mercury, gases given off from new carpeting, furniture made from either wafer or particle board, household solvents and some foam insulations installed up until the late 1970s but which remain in use, are health hazards. Their negative health effects include respiratory ailments, the risk of cancer, and lead or mercury poisoning. Women, of course, are not the only ones susceptible to these illnesses. Men and children are also susceptible. Many exterior and interior paints still contain lead and/or mercury. Paints with mercury give off vapours to which children are particularly vulnerable. Paints with lead taste sweet, and, when it peels off walls or woodwork, may be eaten by small children.

Simon and Eitzen (1986) also indicate a problem with food additives and other products added to drinking water and tooth paste. Food additives, such as nitrates, BHT, BHA, sodium benzoate and benzoic acid, are suspected of causing cancer. Aluminum, used in the form of alum to prevent table salt from caking, is suspected of contributing to alzheimer disease. Fluoride added to toothpaste and municipal water supplies with assurances from manufacturers that the product is safe is also suspected of causing cancer. Similarly, chlorine, also added to municipal drinking water causes cancer.

Again, concern about women's reproductive functions has also resulted in the marketing of products which create hazards to women's health: tampons and the IUD. For many women, tampons are a preferred alternative to napkins or pads. Unfortunately, they can also create a condition known as toxic shock. A deadly illness, toxic shock is caused by staphylococcus bacteria from the vagina or cervix entering the uterus then the bloodstream. Tampons are thought to provide an environment for the proliferation of the bacteria and their resultant toxins. Symptoms of toxic shock include a skin rash, and peeling of thin layers of skin from the body. It also affects the kidneys, liver, intestines, stomach and skin. In many cases, toxic shock is first detected as flu like symptoms followed by a rash. Women who have had vaginal, cervical, or uterine surgery, or have given birth should not use tampons until completely healed.

On a less hazardous note, many manufacturers also market deodorant or scented pads and tampons. Although these products contain no noticeable advantages over soap and water washing, they are marketed as if they do. Marketing strategies attempt to convince women that they are not really clean and fresh unless deodorant pads or tampons are used. In actual fact, the chemicals used in these products can cause skin allergies.

One of the most infamous cases of marketing an unsafe product centred on the marketing of Intra-Uterine Devices (IUDs) such as the Dalkon Shield. Pappert (1986) explains that the Dalkon Shield was simply one of a long list of IUD devices. The first such devices were marketed in Germany around 1909. Their use declined rapidly when they were found to produce infections. While other IUD devices were tested and marketed over the next thirty years, their use had been thoroughly discredited by the 1940s. Concern about rapid population growth in the 1960s led to the reintroduction of a search for an effective IUD. At that time an organization known as the Population Council began a campaign to reconvince the medical profession that IUDs were safe. They pointed to physicians in Japan and Israel who claimed that their patients were using the devices without the negative results of earlier IUDs. Pharmaceutical companies quickly entered the market with new IUDs that they claimed eliminated earlier concerns about infection.

Unfortunately, the new IUDs did not eliminate infection. They also caused pelvic inflammatory disease (PID) and infertility. Previously, PID was associated only with venereal disease. Hence, it came as a surprise when it was shown that IUDs also produced PID. IUD users are nine times more likely to develop PID and are twice as likely to become infertile. More than 200,000 women in the U.S. are said to have become infertile after using IUDs. By the time these problems were detected, the manufacturers of the Dalkon Shield were faced with more than 300,000 lawsuits from women claiming to have been harmed by the device. Despite its problems, there are still some manufacturers and other population control crusaders who promote their use.

Theories of Corporate Violence

Because corporate violence against women is a relatively new research subject, there have been comparatively few attempts to explain it. Nonetheless, some efforts have been made, and these will be reviewed here.

General Theories of Corporate Violence

General theories of corporate violence portray it as a product of corporate profiteering, or as a product of corporate profiteering and individual goal setting. For example, Simon and Eitzen (1986) see it as rooted in efforts of the economic elite's attempts to strengthen and concentrate power. They argue that the concentration of corporate power in relatively few hands gives the corporate elite tremendous influence over the political elite. This influence comes in several forms, including the financing of political campaigns, the selection of political candidates, and the ability to hire and use lobbyists as a means of influencing government decisions. Some corporate elites also become members of the political elite, thereby solidifying the ties.

The result of this merging of the corporate and political elites is that the economic agenda for society, as well as government decision making, including occupational health and safety laws, favours the corporate need for profit making. In this context, corporate violence is a mechanism for generating corporate profits. The violence perpetrated by corporations on women is simply an extension of the overall need to make profits.

Frank (1985), on the other hand, argues that corporate violence in the workplace may be influenced by corporate profit motives, but corporations have goals other than profit. These other goals include prestige, growth and stability. Further, these corporate objectives interact with individual motives, such as success, to make work easier and to achieve job security. In this context, corporate objectives are interpreted by individuals in such a manner as to create situations where individuals place corporate objectives ahead of personal safety. In order to meet their individual goals of success and job security, as well as the corporate goals of profit, growth and stability, corporate personnel may make take risks with their own health, the health of other workers, or even the health of consumers. In this context, corporate violence against women is simply another instance in which corporate and individual goals interact.

Critique

These theories suffer from an obvious problem. While they offer good assessments of corporate capitalism's influence over creation of hazardous working conditions, and even of the production of consumer hazards, they are limited by their failure to consider corporate violence against women as anything other than an extension of general corporate violence. They ignore the significance of patriarchy.

A Theory of Corporate Paternalism

Reasons et al., (1981) propose a theory of corporate violence against women that attempts to deal with the complexities of the merging of corporate capitalism with the forces of paternalism and the division of labour by sex.

> The neglect of women in the workforce generally, and their health and safety needs specifically, reflects such factors as a history of paternalism, lack of occupational alternatives, composition of women in the labour force, degree of unionization, changes in labour demands, and the ideological bias of workmen's compensation boards (1981: 81).

In their vision, corporate capitalism sets the general framework for corporate violence, while these additional factors provide the context for corporate violence against women. Essentially, women's health concerns are seen to be less important, so therefore they are given less attention. The extent to which women unionize into predominantly female unions, and the extent to which those unions place women's health concerns on the bargaining table, determines the seriousness with which women's health concerns are taken. Non-union workplaces, or male dominated unions are less likely to pay attention to women's health needs.

Critique

Just as Simon and Eitzen, as well as Frank, gave too much attention to corporate capitalism, Reasons et al., fail to offer an adequate assessment of influence of patriarchy. They never address the issue of the influence of patriarchy directly. At best, they point out that a division of labour by sex exists, but they do not present a full blown theory of that division of labour. They imply that the division of labour is a product of ideological forces. The division of labour by sex, patriarchy, is not simply an ideological force. It is a separate mode of production demanding to be assessed on its own terms as well as in terms of its interaction with capitalism. This needs to be made clearer in Reasons et al.'s analysis.

Feminist Theory

At this point in time, few feminists have attempted to generate an all embracing theory of corporate violence against women. In most instances, explanations of this problem are offered on a case by case basis. That is, explanations are offered for particular instances or types of corporate violence toward women. For example, sexual harassment is explained as a form of sexual assault. It is a mechanism used to control women. Consequently, this section attempts to combine various trends in feminist investigations of particular forms of corporate violence into a coherent whole.

The key to understanding feminist theory on corporate violence toward women is the observation that women have been and continue to be excluded from the major economic and political decision making bodies of society: the board rooms of major corporations and government. Further, while women are making gains in the labour movement, this movement is still dominated by men. Consequently, decision making within each of these structures is still characterized by institutionalized sexism. Within patriarchal societies, women's concerns about their health and safety, and the health of their children, are not as important as male concerns about profit making and the domination of women.

As a result, women have to turn to alternative structures to inform themselves of the hazards they encounter in the labour force and as consumers. For example, Tudiver (1986) argues that the establishment of women's health networks, in Canada and around the world, have helped women spread the word that certain products were and are hazardous to their health. Without the development of these networks, drugs and medical devices, such as the IUD, would be marketed without resistance. These networks aide the process by which women in third world countries become aware of the dangers of using EP drugs as tests for pregnancy, etc. They inform third world women that IUDs are not a safe form of contraception. They also provide women with information on alternative health care options.

Similarly, women in the labour movement sometimes find it necessary to form unions outside the domain of the male dominated labour movement. Male workers have historically sought to protect their own positions in the labour force, and have, as a result, frequently lobbied to keep women out. In some instances, even though men faced the same risks, male dominated unions have gone along with or lobbied for exclusion of women from some occupations on the grounds that these occupations posed dangers to women's health. The labour movement has also not fought to unionize female workers in situations where labour law makes it difficult to form a union. As Armstrong and Armstrong (1983) observe, where women have organized labour unions they have been more effective in reducing health and safety risks than in those situations where they have not organized. By not seeking to amend the labour laws, and by not attempting to organize unions in situations made difficult by unjust laws, the labour movement serves by default the interest of patriarchy.

So long as women remain outside the decision making process, corporations will continue to market unsafe consumer products, government decision making will continue to allow unsafe products and work conditions, and the labour movement will pay less attention to the concerns of working women than they do to the concerns of working men.

An Alternative Explanation

Corporate violence against women must be viewed as a product of both male domination and capitalist exploitation. It is pointless to deny that corporate violence against women is an extension of the pattern of male domination that characterizes all of Canadian society. Sexual harassment on the job is clearly an extension of the pattern of sexual assault women experience in other areas of their lives. Drugs which give women the illusion of control over their reproductive systems, but which in fact have devastating impact on their health and the health of their children are marketed more for the purpose of profit making than they are for the purpose of giving women control of reproduction. Indeed, as Duggan (1986: 165) explains, the use of birth control technology has little to do with giving women control of their reproductive systems:

In the end, the technology which allows control of reproduction confers power upon its users only when they have enough information to make truly informed choices.

The information needed to allow women to make informed decisions is frequently suppressed or inaccurately described.

The same may be said of the situation encountered by women who work under hazardous conditions. To the extent women workers are given false or misleading information about the technology they are using, and to the extent that they have little or no control over working conditions, female workers are disempowered in the workplace. This leaves them at greater risk of injury and illness.

It is also pointless to deny that, with the possible exception of sexual harassment, men face these same hazards. They encounter threats to their reproductive systems as a result of exposure to various toxic substances. They risk contracting cancer and other illness as a result of working with or near toxic substances or as a result of using unsafe consumer products, etc. They too are the victims of the corporate need to make profit. No one is immune to these problems.

Policy Implications

That workplaces and the market place are hazardous is not new. Concern about occupational health and safety was common during the early years of the industrial revolution, and issues of consumer safety clearly fuelled much of the debate on the need for effective control of the corporate world during the late 1800s and early 1900s (Coleman, 1985; Goff and Reasons, 1978; Pearce, 1973). This section concentrates on various legal and social efforts needed to combat corporate violence against women.

More Restrictive Guidelines on Use and Exposure

Exposure standards set by governments, or by industry, have long been challenged as not offering sufficient protection to exposed workers. For example, in Canada, the Atomic Energy Control Board, which regulates radiation exposure levels, has set the annual maximum radiation exposure level at five rems for all workers. That standard, however, was set in the early 1970s. Since then new research suggests that the exposure level should be reduced.[7] For example, the National Research

---

[7]   The information on radiation exposure levels in this paragraph comes from the CBC program *Monitor*, which aired on October 29, 1990.

Council in the U.S. indicates that the risk of cancer among the children of nuclear workers receiving prolonged exposure to low level radiation is three to four times higher than previously suspected. A study released in Britain, known as the Gardner report, found that the children of workers in one British nuclear plant were almost 10 times more likely than the general population to develop leukaemia. Further, the International Commission on Radiological Protection said in February, 1990, that exposure levels should be cut in half. In the face of mounting evidence, and via union negotiations, Ontario Hydro has set its standard to only 1.8 rems per year. Union negotiators are attempting to lower the standard even further. It must be remembered that the Ontario Hydro standard is voluntary, and the Canadian standard remains at 5 rems per year.

Voluntary guidelines, which are often determined by the industry, are not needed. Instead, mandatory standards, which apply in all provinces, should be developed. At the present time, some workplace health and safety issues are regulated by provincial statute. Thus, the same standard for exposure often differs from one province to another. This has sometimes led to the accusation that corporations with little or no concern for the health or safety of its workers locate, whenever possible, in provinces with the most corporate friendly attitudes. This has produced a patchwork of laws and regulations in industries governed by provincial jurisdiction. Thus, not only must exposure levels to all toxic or potentially toxic substances need to be reduced, but national exposure standards are needed.

Exclusionary Policies

Employer and legal regulations prohibiting women from working in situations where they might be exposed to risks to their reproductive systems have been in effect for most of this century. For example, the hazardous effects of lead on women's reproductive systems was well known by the end of the last century, and by 1919 every government in Europe regulated women workers' exposure to lead. Germany was the first to do so in 1898. Similar laws were also created in the U.S. during the 1930s. These laws usually prohibited women, not men, from working in areas where they would be exposed to lead. As Klein (1987) explains, these laws were created because, women have been and continue to be more closely associated with human reproduction than men. Klein states:

The unspoken assumption underlying such exclusionary policies seems to be that reproduction is primarily women's responsibility.

Thus more sophisticated information on the maternal-fetal relationship and the crossover of substances through the placenta has strengthened exclusionary policies toward women, whereas information on the male contribution to chromosomal and mutagenic changes has not resulted in the exclusion of men (1987: 115).

Even though men also risk damage to their reproductive systems, including damager to sperm, cancer, etc., they were not prohibited from working in high risk areas.

Consequently, where these laws existed, and where they are still in place, they have been challenged on the grounds that they discriminated against women. In the U.S. and Canada, most of these laws were ruled as discriminatory by court rulings and by decision of human rights commissions during the 1970s and 1980s. In some instances, even male workers challenged the laws, claiming that allowing them to be exposed to reproductive health risks while women were exempt was discrimination against men.

The fact that the so-called protective laws were struck down has not prevented corporations from continuing to prohibit female employees from working in areas where their reproductive health is endangered. Chenier (1982) and Klein (1987) note that some corporations have formulated their own, private policies prohibiting women from working in so called high risk areas. Some demand that women show proof of sterility before being allowed to work where they might be exposed to reproductive health hazards. To gain access to these jobs, some women, and some men, have voluntarily sought sterilization.

Even where laws prohibiting the practice are in place, corporations have justified their exclusionary policies on the assumption that they risk law suits from female employees and their children if either can show evidence that their health has been damaged as a result of exposure to a known toxic substance. If such suits are successful, the corporations claim, they could be forced to make large financial settlements which could cripple the economic viability of the corporation.

This explanation, however, has been challenged. If the policies exist because companies wish to reduce the risk of law suits, why is it generally women and rarely men who are excluded from specific work places? In most instances, substances that threaten women's reproductive health also threaten men's reproductive health—neither is immune. In the fight against exclusionary practices, women workers point out that it would be better to make the workplace safer rather than excluding women from working. Exclusionary practices must be resisted by insisting on reductions in exposure levels, and more vigorous enforcement of both criminal and civil law.

Dealing with Sexual Harassment

That women must frequently quit their jobs in order to avoid sexual harassment is an indication that too little is being done to protect them from this problem. That is why it is encouraging to note that sexual harassment has recently been ruled a compensatable injury under the provisions of the Ontario Worker's Compensation Act (Deverell, 1990). In the case described in Figure 5-1, the woman won the right to be compensated for lost wages and received $48,000 as compensation. The case also established the legal responsibilities of employers who know about but refuse to do anything to stop sexual harassment.

The law alone, however, will not stop sexual harassment. While many employers are now establishing anti-harassment policies, most work places still do not have them. Even some work contexts that have anti-harassment policies do not take women's complaints seriously. The possibility remains that pressure will be put on the female employee to accept either an apology or a reprimand of the offending parties as sufficient redress. While this may bring an end to mild sexual harassment, it is not effective in all cases. As illustrated in Figure 5-1, sexual harassment frequently becomes worse after a woman complains about it. Thus, employers and co-workers must not only be made aware of the legal penalties for sexual harassment, they must be made aware of the human cost. They must be sensitized to the fact that sexual harassment is not humorous, that it is, in effect, a form of sexual assault.

Consequently, employers and even unions must not only establish anti-harassment policies, they must initiate programs whereby male workers become more aware of the human cost. Just as it is important for men to become involved in rethinking their attitudes towards violence against women in the home, and elsewhere, it is essential that men in the workplace become more aware of the consequences of sexual harassment. It is clearly the responsibility of men, as employers and workers, to take the problem more seriously and to begin doing something about it.

Protecting the Worker

In addition to establishing lower exposure levels, there are other workplace solutions to occupational health and safety problems. The risk of injury can be reduced by insisting on a wide range of small reforms. For example, food processing plants can reduce injuries and

FIGURE 5-1

Sexually Harassed Worker Wins Landmark Decision
by Leslie Papp, *Toronto Star*

In a landmark ruling a woman who tried to kill herself after sexual harassment by co-workers has won the right to worker's compensation for emotional suffering.

The decision is believed the first of its kind in Ontario. It gives sexual harassment the same status as an accident on the job that causes an injury.

"This has serious ramifications for women," said Leslie Hardy, staff lawyer for the Women's Legal Education and Action fund. It recognized harassment as a legitimate workplace injury ... "

A handful of men routinely baited her, especially after she was made lead hand in charge of a packing line ... After being presented with the penis carved of soap in November, 1986, she resolved to fight the abuse and complained to her union and to management. Two weeks later she was told if she didn't accept one co-worker's apology, and forget about the matter, other workers would deny the incident had occurred.

"At this point, (she) completely broke down, began to shake involuntarily, and, overcome by panic and anxiety, left the work area" ... The victim received psychiatric treatment and returned in March 1987, but harassment continued and in April, 1988, she suffered another nervous breakdown.

Depressed and overwhelmed by feelings of hopelessness, she took an overdose of her psychiatric medication.

Reprinted with permission - *The Toronto Star Syndicate.*

RSI by reducing the speed of the conveyer belts and by allowing more frequent breaks. In other settings, injuries and illness may be reduced by making sure that protective shielding is in place around saws, or other machinery parts which could injure workers. The list is almost endless, and somewhat idealistic.

The fact of the matter is that most of these common sense solutions are already required. What is needed is a greater ability to enforce existing, as well as new safety regulations. This means not only hiring more health and safety inspectors, but also training more workers to take on the responsibility of policing their own workplaces.

With respect to hiring more inspectors, it has long been argued that inspectors frequently cite employee violations of health and safety laws while ignoring employer violations (Reasons et al., 1981). Inspectors often argue that it is pointless to charge employers because these people can resist the charges by engaging in lengthy, and costly court battles. In some instances, inspectors also argue that strict enforcement of safety rules could force some employers to cease operations. What is required, therefore, is not simply more inspectors, but recognition among inspectors that their job is to ensure the health and safety of workers, not necessarily the health of the business.

More and more workers are also becoming aware of the need for on the job safety. The temptation, of course, is to continue working as expected by the employer. In far too many instances this means taking risks that endanger worker safety. The pressure on individual workers to take these risks can be reduced by establishing more occupational health and safety committees in the workplace. These committees need the authority to shut down unsafe workplaces until they are made safe. To avoid abuse of this power, these committees, as is required by law in some provinces, must be composed of both employer and employee representatives. Where disputes can not be settled between the two, government inspectors must be used as arbitrators.

Protecting the Consumer

It is incredible that consumers, male and female, are often victimized by the ability of corporate entities to withhold vital information about the health risks of consumer products. As indicated, some corporations, as in the case of both the drug and asbestos industries, have been fabricating favourable research and suppressing unfavourable data for a long time. What makes this possible is the fact that, as in the drug industry, the marketers of the product are required to show that the product is safe before it can be sold for human consumption. In other situations, such as the chemical industry, products may be sold without any testing for hazardous effects on human health. This is not an easy problem to resolve.

As necessary first steps towards solving the problem, more stringent testing procedures must be initiated. Drugs intended for human use must not only be tested by the manufacturer, they must also be tested by independent agents. Regardless of the industry, the seller makes profits from the sale of the product, and can not be expected to provide unbiased test results. While, the most likely agency to do this job is the government, past experience has shown that even governments frequently permit unsafe products to be sold. Part of the problem is that so many new chemicals are being introduced almost every day that it is impossible with the current limited number of testing agencies to test all of them adequately. It would seem appropriate, therefore, to establish more independent testing agencies. If manufacturers wish to market a new food or drug product, they should be required to pay for independent testing through these agencies before actually marketing the product.

In some cases, of course, product safety does not become an issue until the product has been in use for a prolonged period. It may take prolonged exposure to a substance to reveal that it is harmful. In this case, continuous monitoring of products sold to the consumer is needed.

On a more fundamental level, Simon and Eitzen (1986) argue that the consumer must also accept more responsibility for his/her actions. The consumer bears a responsibility to know as much as possible about the products he/she is using. It is also the consumer's responsibility to begin to reset priorities. Consumers often insist on product qualities, convenience of use, low cost, etc., which potentially compromise safety. A low cost drug is often the result of little testing. Consumers must also become more critical of corporate advertising. Advertising is designed to sell the product by making it appear to be a solution to a problem. In most instances, such as the manufacture, sale and use of some feminine hygiene products, there are clear alternatives. It is also uncertain that these products are needed in the first place.

Finally, as in the case of the establishment of various consumer watch dog groups, such as the women's health networks, it is necessary for consumers to become more active in the process of disseminating product information. Reliance upon either industry or government to provide all needed information is naive. Furthermore, taking responsibility for gathering and disseminating information about consumer products empowers the consumer to take more responsibility for control of his/her health.

Summary

This chapter has concentrated on revealing the various types of corporate violence perpetrated on women. From concerns over occupation health and safety, to issues of consumer safety, it has been shown that women are frequently the victims of deliberate corporate decisions to reduce cost and make profit by sacrificing worker and consumer safety. In exploring explanations for the various types of corporate violence, it was argued that corporate violence against women must be seen as a product of both patriarchy and capitalism. Patriarchy provides the rational for exploiting women's health for profit, while capitalism provides a wider context within which women are exploited not just as women but as workers. The various solutions to the problems discussed in this chapter range from the idealistic expectations that workers and consumers become more involved in taking responsibility for their safety, to concrete suggestions for reform of laws governing workplace and consumer safety. What is perhaps most disturbing is the observation that many of the problems workers and consumers face as we enter the 1990s have existed for more than a century. Indeed, some are as old or older than the industrial revolution itself.

6

CONCLUSION

The main objective of this book has been to sensitize readers to the multidimensional nature of woman abuse in Canada. The sociological literature reviewed throughout this text, although hardly exhaustive, clearly shows that many women are psychologically, sexually, and physically victimized by a broad range of male behaviours that occur in many social contexts, such as within intimate relationships, on the streets, and in the workplace. We have provided ample evidence to support the argument that "women's lives rest upon a continuum of unsafety" (Stanko, 1990: 85).

As the various studies on patterns of abuse reviewed previously demonstrate, all Canadian women are not at equal risk of being abused. Victimization is contingent upon a person's sociodemographic characteristics, physical abilities, or sexual orientation. Nevertheless, most women believe, and rightfully so, that they are potential targets of many types of abuse. As Stanko (1990: 85) points out:

> For the most part, women find that they must constantly negotiate their safety with men—those with whom they live, work and socialize, as well as those they have never met. Because women are likely to be physically smaller than men, as well as emotionally and economically dependent on them, they must bargain safety from a disadvantaged position. As men are likely to be women's intimate companions and their colleagues and bosses at work, the very people women turn for protection are the ones who pose the greatest danger.

While the abusive behaviours discussed earlier threaten many women's physical, psychological, and economic well-being, there are many other dangers that need to be examined by Canadian sociologists.

Our rationale for focusing on a limited number of problems is twofold. First, we wanted to give a small number of issues in depth coverage. A broader-based overview of woman abuse in Canada would not have allowed us to provide more than superficial analyses of a wide range of topics.[1] Second, many significant crimes against women have not been studied in this country. Hence, we would have had to critique research conducted in other nations and thus our work would not have had a decidedly Canadian focus.

Our rationale should not be used, however, to justify further selective inattention given to other dangerous male behaviours that are used to control, degrade, and intimidate women. In the discussion that follows, we will briefly describe some of these threats to women's safety. Hopefully, they will receive more detailed coverage by Canadian sociologists in the near future.

Obscene Phone Calls and Other Types of Non-violent Sexual Assault

The telephone, a necessary instrument of communication for most Canadians,[2] is also a frightening "tool of sexual intimidation" for many women (Stanko, 1990). In England, for example, the British Crime Survey found that approximately 10 percent of females who had access to private phones received obscene calls, and some respondents were victimized many times (Pease, 1985). Generally referred to by the police and phone companies as "nuisance calls" (Stanko, 1990),[3] these "intimate intrusions" (Stanko, 1985) are hardly trivial because they induce a fearful state in a large number of victims (DeKeseredy and Schwartz, in press-a).

There is a lack of empirical research on obscene phone calls. Moreover, the information that has been collected is "tantalizingly sketchy" (Pease, 1985). Nevertheless, exploratory data gathered by the British Crime Survey reveal that there is no association between receiving ob-

---

[1] York University sociologist Desmond Ellis (1987a) refers to this problem as the "cafeteria concept."

[2] More than 99 percent of Toronto households, for example, have at least one phone (Statistics Canada, 1986; Smith, 1990).

[3] The police do not take the victims of obscene phone calls seriously because the callers' behaviours are considered "minor" (DeKeseredy and Schwartz, in press-a). Furthermore, some criminal justice officials refer to them as the normal actions of virile men (Radford, 1987).

scene phone calls and actually being a victim of a physical or sexual assault. This finding may be valid; however, many people do not know how a phone call will end. It is only in retrospect that a caller's intrusion can be designated as insignificant (Kelly and Radford, 1987). At the time of a terrifying call, many women think that the perpetrators will act upon their abusive threats. This is not a irrational perception because some rapists follow up their assaults with phone calls (Stanko, 1990).

In addition to receiving obscene phone calls, many women experience male attacks or sexual advances in public settings which are not usually defined by the state as criminal. Referred to by British left realists as acts of "non-criminal street violence" (Jones et al., 1986), leers, suggestive comments, being followed for blocks down the street, being yelled at from cars, unwanted sexual advances in restaurants and bars, and other forms of harassment cause a large number of women to worry about their personal safety (Radford, 1987; Stanko, 1990; DeKeseredy and Schwartz, in press-a; DeKeseredy and MacLean, 1991). For reasons described above, fear generated by these "little rapes" (Stanko, 1990) is well-founded. Again, it is only in retrospect that these abusive behaviours are regarded as trivial.

Child Abuse

Non-sexual violence, sexual assaults, and various types of psychological maltreatment are not only directed at adult women. Many female children are also abused by both male strangers and relatives. Unfortunately, most of the sociological research on this issue was done by U.S. researchers (e.g., Finkelhor, 1979, 1984; Gelles and Straus, 1988; Straus and Gelles, 1990; Russell, 1984; 1986). Only a handful of relevant Canadian studies have been conducted, and most of them do not provide accurate survey data (Cole, 1985). To date, the best statistics available are those which were gathered in 1983 by a national Gallup poll conducted for the Committee on Sexual Offenses Against Children and Youth (Badgley, 1984).[4] Much more Canadian research is needed. The same thing can be said about violence inflicted upon prostitutes; a problem often indirectly related to child abuse.

---

[4] See Russell (1986) for criticisms of this study.

Violence against Prostitutes

For some children, running away from home is regarded as a temporary solution to the problem of parental abuse (Badgley, 1984). Unfortunately, many runaways lack money and job skills.[5] Some respond to this crisis by entering prostitution, a profession which puts women at high risk of physical and sexual assault (Lowman, 1988; Hatty, 1989). Many are raped and beaten by clients, pimps, managers, and the police (Milman, 1980; Lowman, 1984; Edwards, 1984; Erbe, 1984; Perkins and Bennett, 1985; Gilfus, 1987). But some prostitutes are more at risk than others. The most vulnerable are those women who belong to the "street trade" (Lowman, 1988) because they tend to work in hidden locations (Hatty, 1989). For example, without the risk of their violent actions being detected, clients are more likely to abuse prostitutes.

While it is important to obtain more accurate data on the extent, distribution, and causes of male violence against prostitutes, more information on the legal response to their victimization is also necessary. So far, most of the research on this problem was done in other countries, such as the U.K. and Australia. Some studies, for example, reveal that abused prostitutes receive little, if any, assistance from legal personnel; even if many women are at risk of being murdered by a serial killer like Peter Sutcliffe the "Yorkshire Ripper" (Hatty, 1989).

Prostitutes' ineligibility for criminal justice assistance is a product of unequal power relations between men and women in patriarchal capitalist society (Radford, 1987). Married women are deemed worthy of some protection from male attacks in public places even though their partners' abuse is generally tolerated (Hatty, 1989).[6] On the other hand, prostitutes violate the dominant societal norms of patriarchal heterosexuality by refusing to be restrained and controlled by individual men. Thus, according to the male dominated police and courts, they are not regarded as deserving of protection and justice as are "decent" or "innocent" married women (Radford, 1987).

Do similar attitudes exist within the Canadian criminal justice system? Are assaults against prostitutes also trivialized here? These two questions

---

[5]   Runaways are not able to collect welfare (Lowman, 1987).

[6]   Radford (1987) and Hatty (1989) argue that the police and courts assume that married men have the right to abuse their wives in order to maintain their power and control. Criminal justice personnel will take beatings and sexual assaults more seriously only if they result in serious physical injuries.

must be answered in the near future. Sociological responses to questions about the abuse of elderly women are also necessary.

Elder Abuse in Domestic Settings

For the purpose of this book, the abuse of elderly family members refers to " ... any act or intentional omission that causes old people suffering, serious psychological disturbance, undue violation of their rights and freedoms or any attack against their person or property" (Brillon, 1987: 72).[7] Although this problem is not a recent development (Brillon, 1987), prior to the 1980s it received little attention in North America (Gelles and Cornell, 1985). Now elder abuse is defined as a major type of intimate violence. This societal response is the product of at least four factors. First, there is an increasing number of elderly people and this has increased public awareness about the problems they experience. Second, since people are living much longer than their ancestors, more middle-aged children than ever before are required to look after their old parents (Brillon, 1987; Gelles, 1985). Third, a larger proportion of elderly people than other age categories vote in elections (Gelles and Straus, 1988). The fourth factor is the growing professional interest in the criminal victimization of the elderly (Leroux and Petrunik, 1989).

How many elderly women are abused by their relatives in Canada? Sociologists have not been able to provide adequate responses to this question. A major problem with all Canadian research to date is that the data are derived from health care professionals (Leroux and Petrunik, 1989).[8] These caregivers can only provide information on cases which come to their attention. Thus, many people "suffer in silence" (Pizzey, 1974). Unlike in the U.S. (Pillemer and Finkelhor, 1988), there has been no attempt here to capture information from the victims themselves.

Generally referred to as the authors of the most reliable study on the incidence of elder abuse, Pillemer and Finkelhor discovered that 3 in 100 older Americans have been physically or verbally assaulted. A higher number would have been obtained if these researchers had included institutionalized people in their sample. Most of the victims were mistreated by family members, and the most likely victim is a woman

---

[7] There is no precise definition of elder abuse. In fact, defining this issue has been the subject of much debate. See Brillon (1987) for more information.

[8] For example, see Shell (1982) and Lamont (1985).

eighty years old or older (Gelles and Straus, 1988). Until Canadian sociologists decide to conduct similar victimization surveys, many cases of elder abuse will remain "behind closed doors" (Straus et al., 1981).

REFERENCES

Adams, D. (1989). Feminist-based interventions for battering men. In P.L. Caesar & L.K. Hamberger (Eds.), *Treating men who batter: Theory, practice, and programs.* New York: Springer.

Adelberg, E., & Currie, C. (Eds.) (1987). *Too few to count: Canadian women in conflict with the law.* Vancouver: Press Gang Publishers.

Ageton, S. (1983). *Sexual assault among adolescents.* Lexington: D.C. Heath.

Amir, M. (1971). *Patterns of forcible rape.* Chicago: University of Chicago Press.

Armstrong, P. (1984). *Labour pains: Women's work in crisis.* Toronto: The Women's Press.

Armstrong, P., & Armstrong, H. (1983). *A working majority: What women must do for pay.* Ottawa: Canadian Advisory Council on the Status of Women.

Baetjer, A. M. (1946). *Women in industry: Their health and efficiency.* Philadelphia: W.B. Saunders.

Badgley, R.F. (1984). *Sexual offences against children Vol. 1.* Ottawa: Ministry of Supply and Services.

Barak, G. (1986). Is America really ready for the Currie challenge? *Crime and Social Justice,* 25, 200–203.

Barak, G. (1991). *Gimme shelter: A social history of homelessness in America.* New York: Praeger.

Bard, M. (1988). *Domestic abuse and the homeless women: Paradigms in personal narratives for organizational strategists and community planners.* Ph.D. thesis. Ann Arbour: University of Michigan.

Barnsley, J. (1985). *Feminist action, institutional reaction: Responses to wife assault.* Vancouver: Women's Research Centre.

Barrett, M. (1980). *Women's oppression today: Problems in Marxist feminist analysis.* Thetford, Great Britain: Thetford Press.

Barrett, S., & Marshall, W.L. (1990). Shattering myths: One in four females and one in either males in Canada are sexually abused. *Saturday Night,* June, 21–25.

Battered Women's Support Services (BWSS). (1983). *Teenage battering.* Vancouver: BWSS.

Becker, H.S. (1987). Outsiders. In E. Rubington & M.S. Weinberg (Eds.), *Deviance: The interactionist perspective.* New York: Macmillan.

Berger, R.J., Searles, P., Salem, R.G., & Pierce, B.A. (1986). Sexual assault in a college community. *Sociological Focus,* 19, 1–26.

Berk, R.A., Berk, S.F., Loseke, D.R., & Rauma, D. (1983). Mutual combat and other family myths. In D. Finkelhor, R.J. Gelles, G.T. Hotaling, & M.A. Straus (Eds.), *The dark side of families: Current family violence research*. Beverly Hills: Sage.

Berk, R., & Newton, P. (1985). Does arrest really deter wife battering? An effort to replicate the findings of the Minneapolis spouse abuse experiment. *American Sociological Review*, 50, 253–262.

Bernard, E. (1982). *The long distance feeling: A history of the telecommunications workers union*. Vancouver: New Star Books.

Bill C–127 Working Group. (1982). *Lobby logistics: Bill C–127*. Broadside. December, 4, 3, 4.

Billingham, R.E. (1987). Courtship violence: The patterns of conflict resolution strategies across seven levels of emotional commitment. *Family Relations*, 36, 283–289.

Blau, P. (1964). *Exchange and power in social life*. New York: John Wiley and Sons.

Blumestein, P., & Schwartz, P. (1983). *American couples*. New York: William Morrow.

Boehringer, G., Brown, D., Edgeworth, B., Hogg, R., & Ramsey, I. (1983). Law and order for progressives? : An Australian response. *Crime and Social Justice*, 19, 2–12.

Bograd, M. (1988). Feminist perspectives on wife abuse: An introduction. In K. Yllo & M. Bograd (Eds.), *Feminist perspectives on wife abuse*. Beverly Hills: Sage.

Bohmer, C. (1977). Judicial attitudes toward rape victims. In D. Chappell, R. Geis & G. Geis (Eds.), *Forcible rape: The crime, the victims and the offender*. New York: Columbia University Press.

Bowker, L. (1983). *Beating wife-beating*. Toronto: Lexington.

Box, S. (1983). *Power, crime, and mystification*. London: Tavistock.

Boyd, N. (1988). *The last dance: Murder in Canada*. Scarborough, Ontario: Prentice-Hall.

Brannigan, A. (1984). *Crimes courts and corrections*. Toronto, Ontario: Holt, Rinehart and Winston.

Breines, W., & Gordon, L. (1983). The new scholarship on family violence. *Signs: Journal of Women in Culture and Society*, 8, 491–453.

Brinkerhoff, M., & Lupri, E. (1988). Interspousal violence. *The Canadian Journal of Sociology*, 13, 407–434.

Brillon, Y. (1987). *Victimization and fear of crime among the elderly*. Toronto: Butterworths.

Browne, A. (1987). *When battered women kill*. New York: Free Press.

Brownmiller, S. (1975). *Against our will: Men, women and rape*. New York: Simon and Schuster.

Burgess, A.W., & Holmstrom, L.L. (1974a). Rape trauma syndrome. *American Journal of Psychiatry*, 131, September.

Burgess, A. W., & Holmstrom, L.L. (1974b). *Rape: Victim of crisis.* Bowie, Md.: Robert J. Brady.

Burgess, A.W., & Holmstrom, L.L. (1976). Rape: Its effect on task performance at varying stages in the life cycle. In M. Walker & S. L. Brodsky (Eds.), *Sexual assault.* Lexington: Lexington Books.

Burris, C.A., & Jaffe, P. (1983). Wife abuse as a crime: The impact of police laying charges. *Canadian Journal of Criminology, 25,* 309–318.

Campbell, J.C. (1985). Beating of wives: A cross-cultural perspective. *Victimology, 10,* 174–185.

Canadian Advisory Council on the Status of Women (CACSW) (1976). *The person papers: Health hazards at work.* Ottawa: CACSW.

Cate, R., Henton, J., Koval, J., Christopher, F.S., & Lloyd, S. (1982). Premarital abuse: A social psychological perspective. *Journal of Family Issues, 3,* 79–90.

Chambliss, W.J., & Seidman, R. (1981). *Law, order and power.* New York: Addison Wesley.

Chan, K. (1978). *Husband-wife violence in Toronto.* Ph.D. thesis. North York: Department of Sociology, York University.

Chappell, D., & Singer, S. (1977). Rape in New York City: A study of material in the police files and its meaning. In D. Chappell, R. Geis, & G. Geis (Eds.), *Forcible rape: The crime, the victim and the offender.* New York: Columbia University Press.

Chenier; N.M. (1983). *Reproductive hazards at work: Men, women and the fertility gamble.* Ottawa: Canadian Advisory Council on the Status of Women.

Chimbos, P. (1978). Marital violence: A study of husband-wife homicide. In K. Ishwaran (Ed.), *The Canadian family.* Toronto: Holt, Rinehart and Winston.

Clark, L., & Lewis, D. (1977). *Rape: The price of coercive sexuality.* Toronto: The Women's Press.

Cohen, L., & Backhouse, C. (1980). Putting rape in its place. *MacLeans,* June 30, 6.

Cohen, S. (1979). Guilt, justice and tolerance: Some old concepts for a new criminology. In D. Downes & P. Rock (Eds.), *Deviance and social control.* London: Martin Robinson.

Cohen, S., & Syme, S.L. (1985). Issues in the study and application of social support. In S. Cohen & S.L. Syme (Eds.), *Social support and health.* Toronto: Academic Press.

Cohen, S., & Wills, T.A. (1985). Stress, social support, and the buffering hypothesis. *Psychological Bulletin, 98,* 310–357.

Cole, S.G. (1985). Child battery. In C. Guberman & M. Wolfe (Eds.), *No safe place: Violence against women and children.* Toronto: Women's Press.

Coleman, J.W. (1985). *The criminal elite: The sociology of white collar crime.* New York: St. Martins Press.

Collins, H. (1984). *Marxism and law.* Toronto: Oxford.

Cormier, B.M., & Simons, S.P. (1969). The problem of the dangerous sexual offender. *Canadian Psychiatric Association Journal, 14.*

Cullen, F.T., Maakestad, W.J., & Cavender, G. (1987). *Corporate crime under attack: The Ford Pinto case and beyond.* Cincinnati: Anderson.

Currie, D.H. (1990). Battered women and the state: From the failure of theory to a theory of failure. *The Journal of Human Justice*, 1(2), 77–96.

Currie, D.H., DeKeseredy, W.S., & MacLean, B.D. (1990). Reconstituting social order and social control: Police accountability in Canada. *The Journal of Human Justice*, 2(1), 29–53.

Currie, D.H., & MacLean, B.D. (in press). Women, men and police: Losing the fight against wife battery in Canada. In D.H. Currie & B.D. MacLean (Eds.), *Rethinking the administration of justice.* Toronto: Garamond.

Currie, E. (1985). *Confronting crime: An American challenge.* New York: Pantheon.

Curtis, L. (1973). Victim precipitation and violent crime. *Social Problems*, 21, 594–605.

Czerny, M., & Swift, J. (1988). *Getting started on social analysis in Canada.* Toronto: Between the Lines Publishing Inc.

Daly, M., & Wilson, M. (1988). *Homicide.* New York: Aldine De Gruyter.

Dankwort, J. (1988). Programs for men who batter: A snapshot. *Vis-A-Vis: A National Newsletter on Family Violence*, 6(2), 1–2.

DeKeseredy, W.S. (1988a). Woman abuse in dating relationships: A critical evaluation of research and theory. *International Journal of Sociology of the Family*, 18, 79–96.

DeKeseredy, W.S. (1988b). *Woman abuse in dating relationships: The role of male peer support.* Toronto: Canadian Scholars' Press.

DeKeseredy, W.S. (1988c). Premarital woman abuse: The multidimensional influence of male peer support. *Sociological Viewpoints*, 4, 44–60.

DeKeseredy, W.S. (1988d). Woman abuse in dating relationships: The relevance of social support theory. *Journal of Family Violence*, 3, 1–13.

DeKeseredy, W.S. (1989a). Woman abuse in dating relationships: An exploratory study. *Atlantis: A Women's Studies Journal*, 14, 55–62.

DeKeseredy, W.S. (1989b). Dating violence: Toward new directions in empirical research. *Sociological Viewpoints*, 5(1), 62–74.

DeKeseredy, W.S. (1989c). Dating life events stress, informational support and premarital woman abuse. *International Journal of Sociology of the Family*, 19, 85–94.

DeKeseredy, W.S. (1990a). Male peer support and woman abuse: The current state of knowledge. *Sociological Focus*, 23(2), 129- 139.

DeKeseredy, W.S. (1990b). Woman abuse in dating relationships: The contribution of male peer support. *Sociological Inquiry*, 60(3), 237–243.

DeKeseredy, W.S. (in press). In defence of self-defence: Demystifying female violence against male intimates. In R. Hinch (Ed.), *Debates in Canadian society.* Toronto: Nelson.

DeKeseredy, W.S., & Kelly, K. (1990). With a little help from their friends: Male peer group dynamics and woman abuse in university dating relationships. Unpublished manuscript. Ottawa: Carleton University.

DeKeseredy, W.S., & MacLean, B.D. (1990). Researching woman abuse in Canada: A left realist critique of the Conflict Tactics Scale. *Canadian Review of Social Policy*, 25, 19–27.

DeKeseredy, W.S., & MacLean, B.D. (1991). Exploring the gender, race and class dimensions of victimization: A left realist critique of the Canadian Urban Victimization Survey. *International Journal of Offender Therapy and Comparative Criminology*, 35, 143–161.

DeKeseredy, W.S., & Schwartz, M.D. (in press-a). British left realism on the abuse of women: A critical appraisal. In R. Quinney & H. Pepinsky (Eds.), *Criminology as Peacemaking*. Bloomington: Indiana University Press.

DeKeseredy, W.S., & Schwartz, M.D. (in press-b). British and U.S. left realism: A critical comparison. *International Journal of Offender Therapy and Comparative Criminology*.

Denzin, N.K. (1984). *On understanding emotion*. San Francisco: Jossey-Bass.

DeSilva, S., & Silverman, R. (1985). Innovations in Canadian crime measurement. Paper presented at the annual meeting of the American Society of Criminology, San Diego.

Dexter, L.A. (1958). A note on the selective inattention in social science. *Social Problems*, 6, 176–182.

Deverell, J. (1990). Woman ridiculed in workplace gets 48,000. *Toronto Star*, November 8, A2.

Direcks, A., & Hoen, E. (1986). DES: The crime continues. In K. McDonnell (Ed.), *Adverse effects: Women and the pharmaceutical industry*. Toronto: The Women's Press.

Dobash, R.E., & Dobash, R. (1979). *Violence against wives*. New York: Free Press.

Dobash, R.E., & Dobash, R. (1988). Research as social action: The struggle for battered women. In K. Yllo & M. Bograd (Eds.), *Feminist perspectives on wife abuse*. Beverly Hills: Sage.

Duggan, L. (1986). From birth control to population control: Depro-provera in Southeast Asia. In K. McDonnell (Ed.), *Adverse effects: Women and the pharmaceutical industry*. Toronto: The Women's Press.

Dunford, F., Huizinga, D., & Elliott, C. (1990). The role of arrest in domestic assault: The Omaha police experiment. *Criminology*, 28, 183–206.

Dutton, D.G. (1988). *The domestic assault of women: Psychological and criminal justice perspectives*. Toronto: Allyn and Bacon.

Edwards, S.S.M. (1984). *Women on trial*. Manchester: Manchester University Press.

Edwards, S.S.M. (1989). *Policing 'domestic' violence: Women, law and the state*. London: Sage.

Ehrhart, J.K., & Sandler, B.R. (1985). *Campus gang rape: Party games?* Washington, D.C.: Project on the Status and Education of Women, Association of American Colleges.

Ehrlich, S. (1989). *Lisa, Hedda & Joel: The Steinberg murder case*. New York: St. Martin's Press.

Eisenstein, Z. (1980). *Capitalist patriarchy and the case for socialist feminism*. New York: Monthly Review Press.

Eitzen, D.S., & Timmer, D.A. (1985). *Criminology*. New York: John Wiley and Sons.

Elias, R. (1986). *The politics of victimization: Victims, victimology and human rights*. New York: Oxford.

Elliott, D.S. (1989). The evaluation of criminal justice procedures in family violence crimes. In L. Ohlin & M. Tonry (Eds.), *Crime and justice: An annual review of research. Vol. 11, family violence*. Chicago: University of Chicago Press.

Ellis, D. (1987a). *The wrong stuff: An introduction to the sociological study of deviance*. Toronto: Collier Macmillan.

Ellis, D. (1987b). Policing wife-abuse: The contribution made by 'domestic disturbances' to deaths and injuries among police officers. *Journal of Family Violence*, 2, 319–333.

Ellis, D. (1989). Male abuse of a married or cohabiting female partner: The application of sociological theory to research findings. *Violence and Victims*, 4(4), 235–255.

Ellis, D. (in press). Post-separation woman abuse: The contribution of social support. *Victimology*.

Ellis, D., & DeKeseredy, W.S. (1989). Marital status and woman abuse: The DAD model. *International Journal of Sociology of the Family*, 19, 67–87.

Ellis, M. (1986). Judicial interpretations of the new sexual offences in light of the charter of rights and freedoms: An examination of gender-neutrality, discrimination and inequality. Unpublished manuscript.

Erbe, S. (1984). Prostitutes: Victims of men's exploitation and abuse. *Law and Inequality: Journal of Theory and Practice*, 2, 607–623.

Eshleman, J.R. (1978). *The family: An introduction*. Boston: Allyn and Bacon.

Evans, J., & Himelfarb, A. (1987). Counting crime. In R. Linden (Ed.), *Criminology: A Canadian perspective*. Toronto: Holt, Rinehart and Winston.

Fagan, J., Stewart, D., & Hanson, K. (1981). Violent men or violent husbands? Background factors and situational correlates. In D. Finkelhor, R.J. Gelles, G.T. Hotaling, & M.A. Straus (Eds.), *The dark side of families: Current family violence research*. Beverly Hills: Sage.

Faragher, T. (1985). The police response to violence against women in the home. In J. Pahl (Ed.), *Private violence and public policy*. London: Routledge and Kegan Paul.

Feild, H.S., & Bienen, L.B. (1980). *Jurors and rape*. Toronto: Lexington Books.

Fels, L. (1981). *Living together: Unmarried couples in Canada*. Toronto: Personal Library.

Finkelhor, D. (1979). *Sexually victimized children*. New York: Free Press.

Finkelhor, D. (1984). *Child sexual abuse: New theory and research*. New York: Free Press.

Finkelhor, D., Hotaling, G., & Yllo, K. (1988). *Stopping family violence: Research priorities for the coming decade*. Beverly Hills: Sage.

Finkelhor, D., & Yllo, K. (1985). *License to rape: Sexual abuse of wives.* New York: Free Press.

Fleming, T. (1975). *Violent domestic assault.* Master's thesis. Toronto: Center of Criminology, University of Toronto.

Fonow, M. M. (1983). Occupation/steelworker: Sex/female. In L. Richardson & V. Taylor (Eds.), *Feminist frontiers: Rethinking sex, gender and society.* Reading, Mass.: Addison Wesley.

Ford, A. R. (1986). Hormones: Getting out of hands. In K. McDonnell (Ed.), *Adverse effects: Women and the pharmaceutical industry.* Toronto: The Women's Press.

Frank, N. (1985). *Crimes against health and safety.* New York: Harrow and Heston.

Freedman, L. (1985). Wife assault. In C. Guberman & M. Wolfe (Eds.), *No safe place: Violence against women and children.* Toronto: Women's Press.

Frieze, I.H. (1983). Investigating the causes and consequences of marital rape. *Signs: Journal of Women in Culture and Society,* 8, 532–553.

Gaudet, M A. (1984). The victim and the offender: A puzzling relationship—Part 1. *Liason,* 10(7), 4–11.

Gebhard, P.H., Gagnon, J.H., Pomeroy, W.B., & Christenson, C. V. (1965). *Sex offenders: An analysis of types.* New York: Harper and Row.

Gelles, R.J. (1974). *The violent home.* Beverly Hills: Sage.

Gelles, R.J. (1979). *Family violence.* Beverly Hills: Sage.

Gelles, R.J. (1980). Violence in the family: A review of research in the seventies. *Journal of Marriage and the Family,* 42, 873–885.

Gelles, R.J. (1982). Domestic criminal violence. In M.E. Wolfgang & N.E. Weiner (Eds.), *Criminal violence.* Beverly Hills: Sage.

Gelles, R.J., & Cornell, C.P. (1985). *Intimate violence in families.* Beverly Hills: Sage.

Gelles, R.J., & Straus, M.A. (1988). *Intimate violence: The causes and consequences of abuse in the American Family.* New York: Simon and Schuster.

Gilfus, M.E. (1987). Life histories of women in prison. Paper presented at the Third National Family Violence Conference, Durham, New Hampshire.

Goff, C.H., & Reasons, C.E. (1978). *Corporate crime in Canada: A critical analysis of anti-combines legislation.* Scarborough: Prentice-Hall.

Goff, C.H., & Reasons, C.E. (1986). Organizational crimes against employees, consumers, and the public. In B. MacLean (Ed.), *The political economy of crime: Readings for a critical criminology.* Scarborough, Ontario: Prentice-Hall.

Goffman, E. (1961). *Asylums: Essays on the social situation of mental patients and other inmates.* New York: Anchor.

Gorrie, P. (1990). Victim of harassment told she shares blame. *Toronto Star,* January 23, D1.

Griffin, S. (1971). Rape: The all-American crime. *Ramparts,* 10(3), 26–35.

Gross, B. (1982). Some anticrime proposals for progressives. *Crime and Social Justice,* 17, 51–54.

Groth, N. (1979). *Men who rape.* New York: Plenum Press.

Gunn, R., & Minch, C. (1988). *Sexual assault: The dilemma of disclosure, the question of conviction.* Winnipeg: The University of Manitoba Press.

Gwartney-Gibbs, P., & Stockard, J. (1989). Courtship aggression and mixed-sex peer groups. In M.A. Pirog-Good & J.E. Stets (Eds.), *Violence in dating relationships: Emerging social issues.* New York: Praeger.

Habermas, J. (1975). *Legitimation crisis.* Boston: Beacon Press.

Hagan, J. (1985). *Modern criminology: Crime, criminal behaviour, and its control.* Toronto: McGraw-Hill.

Hanmer, J., & Saunders, S. (1984). *Well-Founded fear: A community study of violence to women.* London: Hutchinson.

Hanmer, J., & Stanko, E.A. (1986). Stripping away the rhetoric of protection: violence to women, law and the state in Britain and the U.S.A. *International Journal of Sociology of the Law,* 13, 357–374.

Harding, J. (1986). Mood-modifiers and elderly women in Canada: The medicalization of poverty. In K. McDonnell (Ed.), *Adverse effects: Women and the pharmaceutical industry.* Toronto: The Women's Press.

Harman, L. (1989). *When a hostel becomes a home: Experiences of women.* Toronto: Garamond Press.

Hatty, S.E. (1989). Violence against prostitute women: Social and legal dilemmas. *Australian Journal of Social Issues,* 24(4), 235–248.

Henton, J., Cate, R., Koval, J., Lloyd, S., & Christopher, S. (1983). Romance and violence in dating relationships. *Journal of Family Issues,* 4, 467–482.

Hinch, R.(1985). Canada's new sexual assault laws: A step forward for women? *Contemporary Crises,* 9(1), 33–44.

Hinch, R. (1988a). The enforcement of Canada's sexual assault law: An exploratory study. *Atlantis,* 14(1), 109–115.

Hinch, R. (1988b). Inconsistencies and contradictions in Canada's sexual assault law. *Canadian Public Policy,* XIV(3), 282- 294.

Hinch, R. (in press). Contradictions, conflicts and dilemmas in Canada's sexual assault law. In G. Barak (Ed.), *Crimes of the capitalist state: The politics of governmental control.* New York: State University of New York Press.

Hindelang, M., & Davis, B.J. (1977). Forcible rape in the United States. In D. Chappell, R. Geis, & G. Geis (Eds.), *Forcible rape: The crime, the victim and the offender.* New York: Columbia University Press.

Hindelang, M., Gottfredson, M., & Garafalo, J. (1978). *Victims of personal crime: An empirical foundation for a theory of personal victimization.* Cambridge, Mass: Ballinger.

Hindelang, M., Hirschi, T., & Weis, J. (1981). *Measuring delinquency.* Beverly Hills: Sage.

Hirschi, T. (1969). *Causes of delinquency.* Berkeley, CA: University of California Press.

Hornung, C.A., McCullough, B.C., & Sugimoto, T. (1981). Status relationships in marriage: Risk factors in spouse abuse. *Journal of Marriage and the Family,* 43, 675–692.

Hotaling, G.T., & Sugarman, D.B. (1986). An analysis of risk markers and husband to wife violence: The current state of knowledge. *Violence and Victims*, 1, 101–124.

Jackman, N. (1982). Bill C–53 law reflects values. *Canadian Women's Studies*, 3(4).

Jaffe, P., Wolfe, P., Telford, A., & Austin, G. (1986). The impact of police charges in incidents of wife abuse. *Journal of Family Violence*, 1, 37–48.

Johnson, H. (1990). Wife abuse. In C. McKie & K. Thompson (Eds.), *Canadian social trends*. Toronto: Thompson Educational Publishing.

Johnson, H., & Chisholm, P. (1990). Family homicide. In C. McKie & K. Thompson (Eds.), *Canadian social trends*. Toronto: Thompson Educational Publishing.

Johnson, L. (1974). The political economy of Ontario women in the nineteenth century. In J. Acton, P. Goldsmith & B. Shepard (Eds.), *Women at work: Ontario 1850–1930*. Toronto: Women's Press Publications.

Jones, T., MacLean, B., & Young, J. (1986). *The Islington crime survey*. Aldershot, England: Gower.

Kanin, E.J. (1967). Reference groups and sex conduct norm violation. *Sociological Quarterly*, 8, 495–504.

Kanin, E.J. (1984). Date rape: Unofficial criminals and victims. *Victimology*, 9, 95–108.

Kanin, E.J. (1985). Date rapists: Differential sexual socialization and relative deprivation. *Archives of Sexual Behaviour*, 14, 219–231.

Karmen, A. (1990). *Crime victims: An introduction to victimology*. Pacific Grove, CA: Brooks/Cole.

Kelly, L., & Radford, J. (1987). The problem of men: Feminist perspectives on sexual violence. In P. Scraton (Ed.), *Law, order and the authoritarian state: Readings in critical criminology*. Philadelphia: Open University Press.

Kennedy, L., & Dutton, D.G. (1989). The incidence of wife assault in Alberta. *Canadian Journal of Behavioural Science*, 21, 40–54.

Kinsey, R., Lea, J., & Young, J. (1986). *Losing the fight against crime*. London: Basil Blackwell.

Klein, P. V. (1987) 'For the good of the race': Reproductive Hazards from lead and the persistence of exclusionary policies towards women. In B. D. Wright, M. M. Ferree, G. O. Mellow, L. H. Lewis, M. D. Smaper, R. Asher, & K. Claspell (Eds.). *Women, work and technology: Transformations*. Ann Arbor: The University of Michigan Press.

Klemmack, S.H., & Klemmack, D.J. (1976). The social definition of rape. In M.H. Walker & S. Brodsky (Eds.), *Sexual assault: The victim and the rapist*. Lexington: Lexington Books.

Koenig, D.J. (1987). Conventional crime. In R. Linden (Ed.), *Criminology: A Canadian perspective*. Toronto: Holt, Rinehart and Winston.

Koss, M.P., Gidycz, C.A., & Wisniewski, N. (1987). The scope of rape: Incidence and prevalence of sexual aggression and victimization in a national sample of students in higher education. *Journal of Consulting and Clinical Psychology*, 55, 162–170.

Koss, M.P., & Oros, C.J. (1982). Sexual experiences survey. A research instrument investigating sexual aggression and victimization. *Journal of Consulting and Clinical Psychology*, 50, 455–457.

LaCheen, C. (1986). Population Control and the pharmaceutical industry. In K. McDonnell (Ed.), *Adverse effects: Women and the pharmaceutical industry*. Toronto: The Women's Press.

LaFree, G.D. (1989). *Rape and criminal justice: The social construction of sexual assault*. Belmont: Wadsworth Publishing Company.

Lamont, C. (1985). La violence à domicile faite aux femmes âgées. Travail présenté pour le Cour EAN 6670: "Condition Féminine et éducation continue." Université de Montréal.

Landau, R., & Lowenberger, L. (1983). Rape law still in crisis. *Broadside*, 4(8), 4.

Laner, M.R. (1983). Courtship abuse and aggression: Contextual aspects. *Sociological Spectrum*, 3, 69–83.

Laner, M.R., & Thompson, J. (1982). Abuse and aggression in courting couples. *Deviant Behaviour*, 3, 229–244.

LaPrairie, C. (1983). *Family violence in rural, northern communities: A proposal for research and program development*. Ottawa: Solicitor General of Canada.

Last, J.M. (1983). *A dictionary of epidemiology*. New York: Oxford.

Lea, J., & Young, J. (1984). *What is to be done about law and order?* New York: Penguin.

Lempert, R. (1989). Humility is a virtue: On the publicization of policy-relevant research. *Law and Society Review*, 23(1), 145–161.

Leroux, T.G., & Petrunik, M. (1989). The construction of elder abuse as a social problem: A Canadian perspective. Paper presented at the annual meeting of the Society for the Study of Social Problems, Berkeley, California.

Levine, M., & Perkins, D.V. (1980). Tailor making life events scale. Paper presented at the annual meeting of the American Psychological Association, Montréal.

Levinson, D. (1989). *Family violence in cross-cultural perspective*. Newbury Park, CA: Sage.

Lewin, B. (1982). Unmarried cohabitation: A marriage form in a changing society. *Journal of Marriage and the Family*, 44, 763–773.

Lewis, C., Agrad, R., Gopic, K.J., Harding, J., Singh, T.S., & Williams, R. (1989). *The report of the race relations and policing task force*. Toronto: Solicitor General of Ontario.

Lott, B., Rielly, M.E., & Howard, D.R. (1982). Sexual assault and harassment: a campus community case study. *Signs: Journal of Women in Culture and Society*, 8(2).

Lowenberger, L., & Landau, R. (1982). A rape by any other name. *Broadside*, 3(9), 3.

Lowman, J. (1984). *Vancouver field study of prostitution*. Working papers on pornography and prostitution, No. 8. Ottawa: Department of Justice.

Lowman, J. (1987). Taking young prostitutes seriously. *The Canadian Review of Sociology and Anthropology*, 24(1), 99- 116.

Lowman, J. (1988). Street prostitution. In V.F. Sacco (Ed.), *Deviance: Conformity and control in Canadian society*. Scarborough, Ontario: Prentice-Hall.

Lupri, E. (1990). Male violence in the home. In C. McKie & K. Thompson (Eds.), *Canadian social trends*. Toronto: Thompson Educational Publishing.

Lupri, E., & Price, M. (1990). Wife abuse across the life course. Paper presented at the annual meeting of the Canadian Sociology and Anthropology Association, Victoria, B.C.

Lynch, M.J., & Groves, W.B. (1989). *A primer in radical criminology*. New York: Harrow and Heston.

MacKinnon, C.A. (1982). Feminism, Marxism, method and the state: An agenda for theory. *Signs*, 7, 3.

MacLean, B.D. (1986). Critical criminology and some limitations of traditional inquiry. In B.D. MacLean (Ed.), *The political economy of crime: Readings for a critical criminology*. Scarborough, Ontario: Prentice-Hall.

MacLean, B.D., & DeKeseredy, W.S. (1990). Taking working class victimization seriously: The contribution of left realist surveys. *International Review of Modern Sociology*, 20, 211–228.

MacLeod, L. (1980). *Wife battering in Canada: The vicious circle*. Ottawa: Advisory Council on the Status of Women.

MacLeod, L. (1987). *Battered but not beaten: Preventing wife battering in Canada*. Ottawa: Advisory Council on the Status of Women.

Makepeace, J.M. (1981). Courtship violence among college students. *Family Relations*, 30, 97–102.

Makepeace, J.M. (1983). Life events stress and courtship violence. *Family Relations*, 32, 101–109.

Makepeace, J.M. (1986). Gender differences in courtship violence. *Family Relations*, 35, 383–388.

Makepeace, J.M. (1987). Social factor and victim-offender differences in courtship violence. *Family Relations*, 36, 87–91.

Mandell, N. (1987). The family. In M.M. Rosenberg, W.B. Shafir, A. Turowetz, & M. Weinfeld (Eds.), *Introduction to sociology*. Toronto: Methuen.

Marcelis, C., & Shiva, M. (1986). EP drugs: Unsafe by any name. In K. McDonnell (Ed.), *Adverse effects: Women and the pharmaceutical industry*. Toronto: The Women's Press.

Marcus, A.M. (1969). Encounters with the dangerous sexual offender. *Canada's Mental Health*, 11.

Maroney, H.J., & Luxton, M. (1987). From feminism and political economy to feminist political economy. In H.J. Maroney & M. Luxton (Eds.), *Feminism and political economy: Women's work, women's struggles*. Toronto: Methuen.

Marshall, W.L. (1973). The modification of sexual fantasies: A combined treatment approach to the reduction of deviant sexual behaviour. *Behavioral Research and Therapy*, 11.

Marshall, W.L., & McKnight, R.D. (1975). An integrated program for sexual offenders. *Canadian Psychiatric Association Journal*, 20.

Matthews, R., & Young, J. (Eds.) (1986). *Confronting crime*. London: Sage.

Maxfield, M. (1984). *Fear of crime in England and Wales*. Home Office Research Study No. 78. London: HMSO.

Mayhew, P., & Hough, M. (1988). The British crime survey: origins and impact. In M. Maguire & J. Pointing (Eds.), *Victims of crime: A new deal*. Philadelphia: Open University Press.

McCahill, T.W., Meyer, L., & Fischman, M. (1979). *The aftermath of rape*. Lexington: Lexington Books.

McDonnell, K. (Ed.) (1986). *Adverse effects: Women and the pharmaceutical industry*. Toronto: Women's Press.

McDonnell, K. (1986). Finding a common ground. In K. McDonnell (Ed.), *Adverse effects: Women and the pharmaceutical industry*. Toronto: The Women's Press.

McNeely, R.L., & Robinson-Simpson, G. (1987). The truth about domestic violence: A falsely-framed issue. *Social Work*, 32, 485–490.

Mead, G.H. (1934). *Mind, self and society*. Chicago: University of Chicago Press.

Media, A., & Thompson, K. (1974). *Against rape*. New York: Farrar, Straus and Giroux.

Megargee, E. (1982). Psychological determinants and correlates of criminal violence. In M.E. Wolfgang and N.A. Weiner (Eds.), *Criminal violence*. Beverly Hills: Sage.

Mercer, S.L. (1988). Not a pretty picture: An exploratory study of violence against women in high school dating relationships. *Resources for Feminist Research*, 17(2), 15- 22.

Messerschmidt, J. (1986). *Capitalism, patriarchy, and crime: Toward a socialist feminist criminology*. Totowa, NJ: Roman and Littlefield.

Michaud, L. (1988). A travesty of justice: How one man's hell became a concern for all. *At the source*, 9(1), 4–6.

Michalowski, R.J. (1983). Crime control in the 1980s: A progressive agenda. *Crime and Social Justice*, 19, 13–23.

Michalowski, R.J. (1985). *Order, law, and crime: An introduction to criminology*. New York: Random House.

Miliband, R. (1969). *The state in capitalist society*. London: Quartet Books.

Mills, C.W. (1959). *The sociological imagination*. New York: Oxford.

Milman, J. (1980). New rules for the oldest profession: Should we change our prostitution laws? *Harvard Women's Law Journal*, 3, 1–35.

Monahan, J. (1981). *Predicting violent behaviour: An assessment of clinical techniques*. Beverly Hills: Sage.

National Institute of Justice. (1986). *Replicating an experiment in specific deterrence: Alternative police response to spouse assault*. Research Solicitation. Washington, D.C.: U.S. Department of Justice.

Nelson, S., & Amir, M. (1977). The hitchhike victim of rape: A research report. In D. Chappell, R. Geis, & G. Geis (Eds.), *Forcible rape: The crime, the victim and the offender.* New York: Columbia University Press.

Nuttall, S.E. (1989). *User report: Toronto sexual assault research study.* Ottawa: Solicitor General of Canada.

Nye, I.F. (1978). Is choice and exchange theory the key? *Journal of Marriage and the family,* 40, 219–233.

Okun, L. (1986). *Woman abuse: Facts replacing myths.* Albany: State University of New York Press.

Pagelow, M.D. (1981). *Woman-battering: Victims and their experiences.* Beverly Hills: Sage.

Pahl, J. (Ed.) (1985). *Private violence and public policy: The needs of battered women and the responses of the public services.* London: Routledge and Kegan Paul.

Papp, L. (1990). Sexually harassed worker wins landmark decision. *Toronto Star,* November 6, A1–2.

Pappert, A. (1986). The rise and fall of the IUD. In K. McDonnell (Ed.), *Adverse effects: Women and the pharmaceutical industry.* Toronto: The Women's Press.

Parliament, J.B. (1990). Women employed outside the home. In C. McKie and K. Thompson (Eds.), *Canadian social trends.* Toronto: Thompson Educational Publishing.

Pearce, F. (1973). Crime, capitalism and the American social order. In I. Taylor & L. Taylor (Eds.), *Politics and deviance.* Harmondsworth: Penguin.

Pease, K. (1985). Obscene telephone calls to women in England and Wales. *The Howard Journal of Criminal Justice,* 24(4), 275– 281.

Pence, E., & Shepard, M. (1988). Integrating feminist theory and practice: The challenge of the battered women's movement. In K. Yllo & M. Bograd (Eds.), *Feminist perspectives on wife abuse.* Beverly Hills: Sage.

Pepinsky, H.E., & Jesilow, P. (1984). *Myths that cause crime.* Cabin John, Maryland: Seven Locks Press.

Perkins, R., & Bennet, G. (1985). *Being a prostitute.* Sydney: Allen and Unwin.

Pfhol, S.J. (1985). *Images of deviance and social control.* Toronto: McGraw-Hill.

Pillemer, K., & Finkelhor, D. (1988). Prevalence of elder abuse: A random sample survey. *The Gerontologist,* 28(1), 51–57.

Pirog-Good, M.A., & Stets, J.E. (Eds.) (1989). *Violence in dating relationships: Emerging social issues.* New York: Praeger.

Pizzey, E. (1974). *Scream quietly or the neighbours will hear.* New York: Penguin.

Pleck, E., Pleck, J.H., Grossman, M., & Bart, P. (1977–78). The battered data syndrome. *Victimology,* 3–4, 680–683.

Pointing, J. & Maguire, M. (1988). Introduction: The rediscovery of the crime victim. In M. Maguire & J. Pointing (Eds.), *Victims of crime: A new deal.* Philadelphia: Open University Press.

Prus, R. (1978). From bar rooms to bedrooms: Towards a theory of interpersonal relations. In A. Bayer-Gammon (Ed.), *Violence in Canada*. Toronto: Methuen.

Quinney, R. (1977). *Class, state and crime: On the theory and practice of criminal justice*. New York: McKay.

Rada, T. (Ed.). *Clinical aspects of the rapist*. New York: Grune and Stratton.

Radford, J. (1987). Policing male violence—Policing women. In J. Hanmer and M. Maynard (Eds.), *Women, violence and social control*. Atlantic Highlands, NJ: Humanities International Press.

Ramkhalawansingh, C. (1974). Women during the great war. In J. Acton, P. Goldsmith, & B. Shepard (Eds.), *Women at work: Ontario 1850–1930*. Toronto: Women's Press Publications.

Ranson, J. (1982a). Past sexual history: The victim on trial. *Kinesis*, November, 5.

Ranson, J. (1982b). Consent and honest belief in C–127. *Kinesis*, October, 12.

Reasons, C.E., Ross, L.L., & Paterson, C. (1981). *Assault on the worker: Occupational health and safety in Canada*. Toronto: Butterworths.

Research and Statistics Group. (1984). *Canadian urban victimization survey, summary report*. Ottawa: Ministry of the Solicitor General.

Rhen, G. (1985). Swedish active labour market policy: Retrospect and prospect. *Industrial Relations*, 24.

Rinehart, J.W. (1987). *The tyranny of work: Alienation and the labour process*. Toronto: Harcourt Brace Jovanovich.

Roscoe, B., & Benaske, N. (1985). Courtship violence experienced by abused wives: Similarities in patterns of abuse. *Family Relations*, 34, 419–424.

Roscoe, B., & Callahan, J.E. (1985). Adolescents self-report of violence in families and dating relations. *Adolescence*, 20, 546–553.

Rosenberg, M. (1968). *The logic of survey analysis*. New York: Basic Books.

Rosenblatt, P.C., & Budd, L.G. (1975). Territoriality and privacy in married and unmarried cohabiting couples. *Journal of Social Psychology*, 97, 67–76.

Russell, D.E.H. (1975). *The politics of rape*. New York: Stein.

Russell, D.E.H. (1982). *Rape in marriage*. New York: Macmillan.

Russell, D.E.H. (1984). *Sexual exploitation: Rape, child sexual abuse, and workplace harassment*. Beverly Hills: Sage.

Russell, D.E.H. (1986). *The secret trauma: Incest in the lives of girls and women*. New York: Basic Books.

Sacco, V. & Johnson, H. (1990). *Patterns of criminal victimization in Canada*. Ottawa: Statistics Canada.

Safilios-Rothschild, C. (1976). A macro- and micro-examination of family power and love: An exchange model. *Journal of Marriage and the Family*, 38, 355–362.

Sanders, W.B. (1980). *Rape and women's identity*. Beverly Hills: Sage.

Saunders, D.G. (1986). When battered women use violence: Husband abuse or self-defense? *Victims and Violence*, 1, 47–60.

Saunders, D.G. (1988). Wife abuse, husband abuse, or mutual combat? A feminist perspective on the empirical findings. In K. Yllo & M. Bograd (Eds.), *Feminist perspectives on wife abuse.* Beverly Hills: Sage.

Saunders, D.G. (1989). Who hits first and who hurts most? Evidence for the greater victimization of women in intimate relationships. Paper presented at the annual meeting of the American Society of Criminology, Reno, Nevada.

Scanzoni, J. (1979). Social process and power in families. In W. Burr et al. (Eds.), *Contemporary theories about the family.* New York: Free Press.

Schechter, S. (1982). *Women and male violence.* Boston: South End Press.

Schulman, M.A. (1979). *A survey of spousal violence against women in Kentucky.* Study No. 792701 conducted for the Kentucky Commission on Women. Washington, DC: U.S. Government Printing Office.

Schur, E.M. (1984). *Labelling women deviant: Gender, stigma and social control.* Philadelphia: Temple University Press.

Schwartz, M.D. (1989). Frat boys will be boys, and occasionally felons. Paper presented at the annual meeting of the Society for the Study of Social Problems, Berkeley, CA.

Schwartz, M.D., & DeKeseredy, W.S. (1988). Liberal feminism on violence against women. *Social Justice,* 15(3–4), 213–221.

Schwartz, M.D., & DeKeseredy, W.S. (1991). Left realist criminology: Strengths, weaknesses and the feminist critique. *Crime, Law and Social Change,* 15, 51–72.

Schwendinger, H., & Schwendinger, J. (1970). Defenders of order or guardians of human rights. *Issues in Criminology,* 7, 72- 81.

Schwendinger, J.R., & Schwendinger, H. (1983). *Rape and inequality.* Beverly Hills: Sage.

Scott, D. (1990). Feminist explanations of wife assault: Coping with diversity in the experiences of battered women and their papers. Paper presented at the annual meeting of the Canadian Law and Society Association, Victoria, B.C.

Scraton, P. (Ed.). (1987). *Law, order and the authoritarian state.* Philadelphia: Open University Press.

Sharp, A.D. (1990). *Violence against women in rural Outaouais: Validation of a screening device and of survey methods: A pilot project.* Report prepared for Conseil Regional Services Sociaux-Sante De L'Outaouais. Quebec: Conseil local des Services Communautaire Vallee-De-La Gatineau.

Shartal, S. (1988). The cutting edge: UFCW members on three fronts of the food industry. *At the Source,* 9(1), 6–9.

Shell, D.J. (1982). *Protection of the elderly: A study of elder abuse.* Manitoba Council on Aging. Winnipeg: Manitoba Association on Gerontology.

Sherman, L., & Berk, R. (1984a). The specific deterrent effects of arrest for domestic assault. *American Sociological Review,* 49, 261–272.

Sherman, L., & Berk, R. (1984b). *The Minneapolis domestic violence experiment.* Washington, D.C.: Police Foundation Reports 1.

Sherman, L., & Cohn, E. (1989). The impact of research on legal policy: The Minneapolis domestic violence experiment. *Law and Society Review*, 23, 117–144.

Siegel, L.J. (1989). *Criminology*. New York: West.

Sigelman, C.K., Berry, C.J., & Wiles, K.A. (1984). Violence in college students'dating relationships. *Journal of Applied Social Psychology*, 5, 530–548.

Silberman, C. (1980). *Criminal violence, criminal justice*. New York: Vintage Books.

Simon, D.R., & Eitzen, D. (1986). *Elite deviance*. Boston: Allyn and Bacon.

Skipper, J.K., & Nass, G. (1966). Dating behaviour: A framework for analysis and an illustration. *Journal of Marriage and the Family*, 28, 412–413.

Small, S. (1981). The interactionist perspective on wife assault: A sociological rule of thumb. Paper presented at the annual meeting of the Canadian Sociology and Anthropology Association, Halifax, Nova Scotia.

Smart, C. (1976). *Women crime and criminology: A feminist critique*. London: Routledge and Kegan Paul.

Smith, D. (1985). Women, class and family. In V. Burstyn & D. E. Smith. *Women, class, family and the state*. Toronto: Garamond Press.

Smith, M.D. (1985). *Woman abuse: The case for surveys by telephone*. The LaMarsh Research Programme on Violence and Conflict Resolution. Report No. 12. North York, Ontario: York University.

Smith, M.D. (1986). Effects of question format on the reporting of woman abuse: A telephone survey experiment. *Victimology*, 11, 430–438.

Smith, M.D. (1987). The incidence and prevalence of woman abuse in Toronto. *Violence and Victims*, 2(3), 173–187.

Smith, M.D. (1988). Women's fear of violent crime: An exploratory test of a feminist hypothesis. *Journal of Family Violence*, 3(1), 29–38.

Smith, M.D. (1989a). *Woman abuse in Toronto: Incidence, prevalence and sociodemographic correlates*. The LaMarsh Research Programme on Violence and Conflict Resolution. Report No. 18. North York, Ontario: York University.

Smith, M.D. (1989b). Woman abuse: The case for surveys by telephone. *Journal of Interpersonal Violence*, 4(3), 308–324.

Smith, M.D. (1990). Sociodemographic risk factors in wife abuse: Results from a survey of Toronto women. *The Canadian Journal of Sociology*, 15(1), 39–58.

Smith, M.D. (in press). Patriarchal ideology and wife beating: A test of a feminist hypothesis. *Violence and Victims*.

Snider, L. (1985). Legal reform and social control: The dangers of abolishing rape. *International Journal of Law*, 13, 337–356.

Snider, L. (1990). The potential of the criminal justice system to promote feminist concerns. *Studies in Law, Politics, and Society*, 10, 141–169.

Solicitor General of Canada. (1983). *Canadian urban victimization survey: Victims of crime*. Ottawa: Ministry of the Solicitor General.

Solicitor General of Canada. (1984a). *Canadian urban victimization survey: Reported and unreported crimes*. Ottawa, Ministry of the Solicitor General.

Solicitor General of Canada. (1984b). *Canadian urban victimization survey: Crime prevention: Awareness and practice.* Ottawa: Ministry of the Solicitor General.

Solicitor General of Canada. (1985a). *Canadian urban victimization survey: Female victims of crime.* Ottawa: Ministry of the Solicitor General.

Solicitor General of Canada. (1985b). *Canadian urban victimization survey: Cost of crime to victims.* Ottawa: Ministry of the Solicitor General.

Solicitor General of Canada. (1985c). *Canadian urban victimization survey: Criminal victimization of elderly Canadians.* Ottawa: Ministry of the Solicitor General.

Solicitor General of Canada. (1986). Reported and unreported crimes. In R. Silverman & J. Teevan (Eds.), *Crime in Canadian society.* Toronto, Butterworths.

Solicitor General of Canada. (1987). *Canadian urban victimization survey: Patterns in violent crime.* Ottawa: Ministry of the Solicitor General.

Solicitor General of Canada. (1988). *Canadian urban victimization survey: Multiple victimization.* Ottawa: Ministry of the Solicitor General.

Sprey, J. (1979). Conflict theory and the study of marriage and the family. In W. Burr et al. (Eds.), *Contemporary theories about the family.* New York: Free Press.

Stanko, E.A. (1985). *Intimate intrusions: Women's experience of male violence.* London: Routledge and Kegan Paul.

Stanko, E.A. (1987). Typical violence, normal precaution: Men, women and interpersonal violence in England, Wales, Scotland, and the U.S.A. In J. Hanmer & M. Maynard (Eds.), *Women, violence and social control.* Atlantic Highlands, NJ: Humanities Press International.

Stanko, E.A. (1988). Fear of crime and the myth of the safe home: A feminist critique of criminology. In K. Yllo & M. Bograd (Eds.), *Feminist perspectives on wife abuse.* Beverly Hills: Sage.

Stanko, E.A. (1989). Missing the mark? Policing battering. In J. Hanmer, J. Radford, & E.A. Stanko (Eds.), *Women, policing, and male violence.* London: Routledge and Kegan Paul.

Stanko, E.A. (1990). *Everyday violence: How women and men experience sexual and physical danger.* London: Pandora.

Stark, E., Flitcraft, A., & Frazier, W. (1979). Medicine and patriarchal violence: The social construction of a 'private' event. *International Journal of Health Services, 9,* 461–492.

Stark-Adamec, C., & Adamec, P. (1982). Aggression by men against women: Adaptation or aberration? *International Journal of Women's Studies, 5,* 42–54.

Statistics Canada (1984). *Homicide in Canada, 1984: A statistical perspective.* Ottawa: Statistics Canada.

Statistics Canada. (1986). *Household facilities and equipment survey, household surveys division.* Unpublished manuscript. Ottawa: Statistics Canada.

Statistics Canada. (1990). *Conjugal violence against women.* Juristat Service Bulletin. Ottawa: Statistics Canada.

Stein, P. (1983). Singlehood. In E. Macklin & R. Rubin (Eds.), *Contemporary families and alternative lifestyles.* Beverly Hills: Sage.

Steinmetz, S.K. (1977–78). The battered husband syndrome. *Victimology,* 3–4, 499–509.

Stets, J.E, & Straus, M.A. (1989). The marriage license as a hitting license: A comparison of assaults in dating, cohabiting, and married couples. In M. Pirog-Good & J.E. Stets (Eds.), *Violence in dating relationships: Emerging social issues.* New York: Praeger.

Stets, J.E., & Straus, M.A. (1990). Gender differences in reporting marital violence and its medical and psychological consequences. In M.A. Straus & R.J. Gelles (Eds.), *Physical violence in American families.* New Brunswick, NJ: Transaction.

Straus, M.A. (1974). Leveling, civility, and violence in the family. *Journal of Marriage and the Family,* 36, 13–30.

Straus, M.A. (1976). Sexual inequality, cultural norms, and wife beating. *Victimology,* 1, 54–76.

Straus, M.A. (1979). Measuring intrafamily conflict and violence: The conflict tactics (CT) scales. *Journal of Marriage and the Family,* 41, 75–88.

Straus, M.A. (1989). Gender differences in assault in intimate relationships: Implications for the primary prevention of spousal violence. Paper presented at the annual meeting of American Society of Criminology, Reno, Nevada.

Straus, M.A. (1990). The conflict tactics scales and its critics: An evaluation and new data on validity and reliability. In M.A. Straus & R.J. Gelles (Eds.), *Physical violence in American families: Risk factors and adaptations to violence in 8,145 families.* New Brunswick, NJ: Transaction.

Straus, M.A., & Gelles, R.J. (1979). Determinants of aggression in the family: Toward a theoretical integration. In W. Burr et al. (Eds.), *Contemporary theories about the family.* New York: Free Press.

Straus, M.A., & Gelles, R.J. (1986). Societal changes and change in family violence from 1975 to 1985 as revealed by two national surveys. *Journal of Marriage and the Family,* 48, 465–479.

Straus, M.A., & Gelles, R.J. (Eds.) (1990). *Physical violence in American families: Risk factors and adaptations to violence in 8,145 families.* New York: Transaction.

Straus, M.A., Gelles, R.J., & Steinmetz, S.K. (1981). *Behind closed doors: Violence in the American family.* New York: Anchor Books.

Straus, M.A., Sweet, S., & Vissing, Y.M. (1989). Verbal aggression against spouses and children in a nationally representative sample of American families. Paper presented at the annual meeting of the Speech Communication Association, San Francisco.

Sugarman, D.B., & Hotaling, G.T. (1989). Dating violence: Prevalence, context, and risk markers. In M. Pirog-Good & J.E. Stets (Eds.), *Violence in dating relationships: Emerging social Issues.* New York: Praeger.

Sutherland. E. (1940). White collar criminality. *American Sociological Review,* 5, 1–12.

Sutherland, E. (1945). Is 'white collar crime' crime? *American Sociological Review*, 10, 132–39.

Tappan, P. W. (1947). Who is the criminal? *American Sociological Review*, 12, 96–112.

Taylor, I. (1981). *Law and order: Arguments for socialism*. London: The Macmillan Press.

Taylor, I. (1982). Against crime and for socialism. *Crime and Social Justice*, 18, 4–15.

Taylor, I. (1983). *Crime, capitalism and community: Three essays in socialist criminology*. Toronto: Butterworths.

Teevan, J. (1987). *Basic sociology: A Canadian introduction*. Toronto: Prentice-Hall.

Toby, J. (1957). Social disorganization and stake in conformity: Complementary factors in the predatory behaviour of young hoodlums. *Journal of Criminal Law, Criminology and Police Science*, 48, 12–17.

Tudiver, S. (1986). The strength of links: International women's health networks in the eighties. In K. McDonnell (Ed.), *Adverse effects: women and the pharmaceutical industry*. Toronto: The Women's Press.

Turcotte, P. (1990). Common-law unions; nearly half a million in 1986. In C. McKie & K. Thompson (Eds.), *Canadian social trends*. Toronto: Thompson Educational Publishing.

Ursel, E.J. (1984). Toward a theory of reproduction. *Contemporary Crises*, 8, 265–292.

Ursel, E.J. (1986). The state and the maintenance of patriarchy: A case study of family, labour and welfare legislation in Canada. In J. Dickinson & B. Russell (Eds.), *Family, economy and state*. Toronto: Garamond.

Ursel, E.J. (1990). Considering the impact of the wife abuse movement on the state: The example of Manitoba. Paper presented at the annual meeting of the Canadian Sociology and Anthropology Association, Victoria, B.C.

Ursel, E.J., & Farough, D. (1986). The legal and public response to the new wife abuse directive in Manitoba. *Canadian Journal of Criminology*, Spring, 171–182.

Walker, G.E. (1990). *Family violence and the women's movement: The conceptual politics of struggle*. Toronto: University of Toronto Press.

Walker, L.E. (1977–78). Battered women and learned helplessness. *Victimology*, 3–4, 525–534.

Walker, L.E. (1979). *The battered woman*. New York: Harper and Row.

Walker, L.E. (1983). The battered women syndrome study. In D. Finkelhor, R.J. Gelles, G.T. Hotaling, & M.A. Straus (Eds.), *The dark side of families: Current family violence research*. Beverly Hills: Sage.

Walklate, S. (1989). *Victimology: the victim and the criminal justice process*. London: Unwin Hyman.

Williams, K.R., & Hawkins, R. (1989). The meaning of arrest for wife assault. *Criminology*, 27, 163–181.

Wills, T.A. (1985). Supportive functions of interpersonal relationships. In S. Cohen & S.L. Syme (Eds.), *Social support and health*. Toronto: Academic Press.

Wolfgang, M.E. (1958). *Patterns in criminal homicide*. Philadelphia: University of Pennsylvania Press.

Yllo, K., & Straus, M.A. (1981). Interpersonal violence among married and cohabiting couples. *Family Relations, 30,* 339- 347.

Young, J. (1979). Left idealism, reformism and beyond: From criminology to Marxism. In B. Fine, R. Kinsey, J. Lea, S. Picciotto, & J. Young (Eds.), *Capitalism and the rule of law*. London: Hutchinson.

Young, J. (1986). The failure of criminology. In R. Matthews & J. Young (Eds.), *Confronting crime*. London: Sage.

Young, K. (1988). Violence in the workplace of professional sport from victimological and cultural studies perspectives. Paper presented at the annual meeting of the North American Society for the sociology of Sport, Cincinnati, Ohio.

Young, K., & Reasons, C.E. (1989). Victimology and organizational crime: Workplace violence and the professional athlete. *Sociological Viewpoints, 5*(1), 24–34.

Zaretsky, E. (1976). *Capitalism, the family and personal life*. New York: Harper and Row.

INDEX

Date Due

APR 0 3 1998		
APR 0 4 1998		
APR 0 9 2000		
APR 0 4 2000		
DEC 1 2 2000		
NOV 2 7 2000		
APR 1 6 2001		
APR 1 6 2001		
NOV 1 9 2001		
NOV 2 9 2001		
OCT 1 7 2002		
NOV 2 2002		
NOV 2 8 2002		
NOV 2 1 2002		
MAR 0 2 2004		
MAR 2 3 2004		
MAR 2 4 2004		
NOV 2 9 2004		
NOV 2 6 2004		
FEB 1 2 2005		
MAR 1 8 2005		

PRINTED IN U.S.A.   CAT. NO. 24 161   BRODART

Printed in Canada